# THE LONELY MAN OF FAITH

JOSEPH B. SOLOVEITCHIK

*The
Lonely
Man
of
Faith*

D O U B L E D A Y

New York   London   Toronto   Sydney   Auckland

PUBLISHED BY DOUBLEDAY
a division of Bantam Doubleday Dell Publishing Group, Inc.
666 Fifth Avenue, New York, New York 10103

DOUBLEDAY and the portrayal of an anchor with a dolphin
are trademarks of Doubleday, a division of
Bantam Doubleday Dell Publishing Group, Inc.

Library of Congress Cataloging-in-Publication Data

Soloveitchik, Joseph Dov.
The lonely man of faith/Joseph B. Soloveitchik.
p.   cm.
1. Faith (Judaism)   2. Loneliness—Religious aspects—Judaism.
I. Title.
BM729.F3S614   1992
296.3—dc20   91-33401
CIP

ISBN 0-385-42262-8

TO TONYA
A woman of great courage, sublime dignity,
total commitment,
and uncompromising truthfulness

The basic ideas of *The Lonely Man of Faith* were formulated in Rabbi Soloveitchik's lectures in the "Marriage and Family" program of the National Institute of Mental Health Project at Yeshiva University in New York City. The essay was first published in the journal *Tradition* in 1965.

Brief notes in the text are listed at the foot of each page. Longer notes are numbered and listed at the end of each Roman-numeral section.

—Ed.

# THE LONELY MAN OF FAITH

IT IS NOT THE PLAN of this essay to discuss the millennium-old problem of faith and reason. Theory is not my concern at the moment. I want instead to focus attention on a human-life situation in which the man of faith as an individual concrete being, with his cares and hopes, concerns and needs, joys and sad moments, is entangled. Therefore, whatever I am going to say here has been derived not from philosophical dialectics, abstract speculation, or detached impersonal reflections, but from actual situations and experiences with which I have been confronted. Indeed, the term "lecture" also is, in this context, a misnomer. It is rather a tale of a personal dilemma. Instead of talking theology, in the didactic sense, eloquently and in balanced sentences, I would like, hesitantly and haltingly, to confide in you, and to share with you some concerns which weigh heavily on my mind and which frequently assume the proportions of an awareness of crisis.

I have no problem-solving thoughts. I do not intend to suggest a new method of remedying the human situation which I am about to describe; neither do I believe that it can be remedied at all. The role of the man of faith, whose religious experience is fraught with inner conflicts and incongruities, who oscillates between ecstasy in God's companionship and despair when he feels abandoned by God, and who is torn asunder by the heightened contrast between self-appreciation and abnegation, has been a difficult one since the times of Abraham and Moses. It would be presumptuous of me to attempt to convert the passional, antinomic faith-experience into a eudaemonic, harmonious one, while the Biblical knights of faith lived heroically with this very tragic and paradoxical experience.

All I want is to follow the advice given by Elihu, the son of Berachel of old, who said, "I will speak that I may find relief"; for there is a redemptive quality for an agitated mind in the spoken word, and a tormented soul finds peace in confessing.

# I

THE NATURE of the dilemma can be stated in a three-word sentence. I am lonely. Let me emphasize, however, that by stating "I am lonely" I do not intend to convey to you the impression that I am alone. I, thank God, do enjoy the love and friendship of many. I meet people, talk, preach, argue, reason; I am surrounded by comrades and acquaintances. And yet, companionship and friendship do not alleviate the passional experience of loneliness which trails me constantly. I am lonely because at times I feel rejected and thrust away by everybody, not excluding my most intimate friends, and the words of the Psalmist, "My father and my mother have forsaken me," ring quite often in my ears like the plaintive cooing of the turtledove. It is a strange, alas, absurd experience engendering sharp, enervating pain as well as a stimulating, cathartic feeling. I despair because I am lonely and, hence, feel frustrated. On the other hand, I also feel invigorated because this very experience of loneliness presses everything in me into the service of God. In my "desolate, howling solitude" I experience a growing awareness that, to paraphrase Plotinus's apothegm about prayer, this service to which I, a lonely and solitary individual, am committed is wanted and gracefully accepted by God in His transcendental loneliness and numinous solitude.

I must address myself to the obvious question: why am I beset by this feeling of loneliness and being unwanted? Is it the Kierkegaardian anguish—an ontological fear nurtured by the awareness of nonbeing threatening one's existence—that assails me, or is this feeling of loneliness solely due to my own personal stresses, cares, and frustrations? Or is it perhaps the result of the pervasive state of mind of Western man who has become estranged from himself, a state with which all of us as Westerners are acquainted?

I believe that even though all three explanations might be true to some extent, the genuine and central cause of the feeling of loneliness from which I cannot free myself is to be found in a different dimension, namely, in the experience of faith itself. I am lonely because, in my humble, inadequate way, I am a man of faith for whom to be means to believe, and who substituted "credo" for "cogito" in the time-honored Cartesian maxim.* Apparently, in this role, as a man of faith, I must experience a sense of loneliness which is of a compound nature. It is a blend of that which is inseparably interwoven into the very texture of the faith gesture, characterizing the unfluctuating metaphysical destiny of the man of faith, and of that which is extraneous to the act of believing and stems from the ever-changing human-historical situation with all its whimsicality. On the one hand, the man of faith has been a solitary figure throughout the ages, indeed millennia, and no one has succeeded in escaping this unalterable destiny which is an "objective" awareness rather than a subjective feeling. On the other hand, it is undeniably true that this basic awareness expresses itself in a variety of ways, utilizing the whole gamut of one's affective emotional life which is extremely responsive to outward challenges and moves along with the tide of cultural and historical change. Therefore, it is my intent to analyze this experi-

---

*This is, of course, a rhetorical phrase, since all emotional and volitional activity was included in the Cartesian *cogitatio* as *modi cogitandi*. In fact, faith in the existence of an intelligent *causa prima* was for Descartes an integral part of his logical postulate system, by which he proves the existence of the external world.

---

ence at both levels: at the ontological, at which it is a root awareness, and at the historical, at which a highly sensitized and agitated heart, overwhelmed by the impact of social and cultural forces, filters this root awareness through the medium of painful, frustrating emotions.

As a matter of fact, the investigation at the second level is my prime concern since I am mainly interested in contemporary man of faith who is, due to his peculiar position in our secular society, lonely in a special way. No matter how time-honored and time-hallowed the interpenetration of faith and loneliness is, and it certainly goes back to the dawn of the Judaic covenant, contemporary man of faith lives through a particularly difficult and agonizing crisis.

Let me spell out this passional experience of contemporary man of faith.

He looks upon himself as a stranger in modern society, which is technically minded, self-centered, and self-loving, almost in a sickly narcissistic fashion, scoring honor upon honor, piling up victory upon victory, reaching for the distant galaxies, and seeing in the here-and-now sensible world the only manifestation of being. What can a man of faith like myself, living by a doctrine which has no technical potential, by a law which cannot be tested in the laboratory, steadfast in his loyalty to an eschatological vision whose fulfillment cannot be predicted with any degree of probability, let alone certainty, even by the most complex, advanced mathematical calculations—what can such a man say to a functional, utilitarian society which is *saeculum*-oriented and whose practical reasons of the mind have long ago supplanted the sensitive reasons of the heart?

It would be worthwhile to add the following in order to place the dilemma in the proper focus. I have never been seriously troubled by the problem of the Biblical doctrine of creation vis-à-vis the scientific story of evolution at both the cosmic and the organic levels, nor have I been perturbed by the confrontation of the mechanistic interpretation of the human mind with the Biblical spiritual concept of man. I have not been perplexed by the impossibility of fitting the mystery of revelation into the framework of historical empiricism. Moreover, I have not even been troubled by the theories of Biblical criticism which contradict the very foundations upon which the sanctity and integrity of the Scriptures rest. However, while theoretical oppositions and dichotomies have never tormented my thoughts, I could not shake off the disquieting feeling that the practical role of the man of faith within modern society is a very difficult, indeed, a paradoxical one.

The purpose of this essay, then, is to define the great dilemma confronting contemporary man of faith. Of course, as I already remarked, by defining the dilemma we do not expect to find its solution, for the dilemma is insoluble. However, the defining itself is a worthwhile cognitive gesture which, I hope, will yield a better understanding of ourselves and our commitment. Knowledge in general and self-knowledge in particular are gained not only from discovering logical answers but also from formulating logical, even though unanswerable, questions. The human logos is as concerned with an honest inquiry into an insoluble antinomy which leads to intellectual despair and humility as it is with an unprejudiced true solution of a complex problem arousing joy and enhancing one's intellectual determination and boldness.

Before beginning the analysis, we must determine within which frame of reference, psychological and empirical or theological and Biblical, our dilemma should be described. I believe you will agree with me that we do not have much choice in the matter; for, to the man of faith, self-knowledge has one connotation only—to understand one's place and role within the scheme of events and things willed and approved by God, when He ordered finitude to emerge out of infinity and the Universe, including man, to unfold itself. This kind of self-knowledge may not always be pleasant or comforting. On the contrary, it might from time to time express itself in a painful appraisal of the difficulties which man of faith, caught in his paradoxical destiny, has to encounter, for knowledge at both planes, the scientific and the personal, is not always a eudaemonic experience. However, this unpleasant prospect should not deter us from our undertaking.

Before I go any further, I want to make the following reservation. Whatever I am about to say is to be seen only as a modest attempt on the part of a man of faith to interpret his spiritual perceptions and emotions in modern theological and philosophical categories. My interpretive gesture is completely subjective and lays no claim to representing a definitive Halakhic philosophy. If my audience will feel that these interpretations are also relevant to their perceptions and emotions, I shall feel amply rewarded. However, I shall not feel hurt if my thoughts will find no response in the hearts of my listeners.

WE ALL KNOW that the Bible offers two accounts of the creation of man. We are also aware of the theory suggested by Bible critics attributing these two accounts to two different traditions and sources. Of course, since we do unreservedly accept the unity and integrity of the Scriptures and their divine character, we reject this hypothesis which is based, like much Biblical criticism, on literary categories invented by modern man, ignoring completely the eidetic-noetic content of the Biblical story. It is, of course, true that the two accounts of the creation of man differ considerably. This incongruity was not discovered by the Bible critics. Our sages of old were aware of it.* However, the answer lies not in an alleged dual tradition but in dual man, not in an imaginary contradiction between two versions but in a real contradiction in the nature of man. The two accounts deal with two Adams, two men, two fathers of mankind, two types, two representatives of humanity, and it is no wonder that they are not identical. Let us just read these two accounts.

In Genesis 1 we read: "So God created man in His own image, in the image of God created He him, male and female created He them. And God blessed them and God said unto them, be fruitful and multiply, and fill the earth and subdue it, and have dominion over the fish of the sea, over the fowl of the heaven, and over the beasts, and all over the earth."

*Vide *Berakhot*, 61a; *Ketuvot*, 8a; Nachmanides, Genesis 2:7; *Cuzari*, IV.

In Genesis 2, the account differs substantially from the one we just read: "And the eternal God formed the man of the dust of the ground and breathed into his nostrils the breath of life and man became a living soul. And the eternal God planted a garden eastward in Eden. . . . And the eternal God took the man and placed him in the Garden of Eden to serve it and to keep it."

I want to point out four major discrepancies between these two accounts:

1. In the story of the creation of Adam the first, it is told that the latter was created in the image of God, בצלם א־לקים, while nothing is said about how his body was formed. In the account of the creation of Adam the second, it is stated that he was fashioned from the dust of the ground and God breathed into his nostrils the breath of life.

2. Adam the first received the mandate from the Almighty to fill the earth and subdue it, מלאו את הארץ וכבשה. Adam the second was charged with the duty to cultivate the garden and to keep it, לעבדה ולשמרה.

3. In the story of Adam the first, both male and female were created concurrently, while Adam the second emerged alone, with Eve appearing subsequently as his helpmate and complement.

4. Finally, and this is a discrepancy of which

Biblical criticism has made so much, while in the first account only the name of E-lohim appears, in the second, E-lohim is used in conjunction with the Tetragrammaton.

LET US PORTRAY these two men. Adam the first and Adam the second, in typological categories.

There is no doubt that the term "image of God" in the first account refers to man's inner charismatic endowment as a creative being. Man's likeness to God expresses itself in man's striving and ability to become a creator. Adam the first who was fashioned in the image of God was blessed with great drive for creative activity and immeasurable resources for the realization of this goal, the most outstanding of which is the intelligence, the human mind, capable of confronting the outside world and inquiring into its complex workings.* In spite of the boundless divine generosity providing man with many intellectual capacities and interpretive perspectives in his approach to reality, God, in imparting the blessing to Adam the first and giving him the mandate to subdue nature, directed Adam's attention to the functional and practical aspects of his intellect through which man

*Vide *Yesode ha-Torah*, IV, 8–9; *Moreh Nevukhim*, I, 1.

is able to gain control of nature. Other intellectual inquiries, such as the metaphysical or axiologico-qualitative, no matter how incisive and penetrating, have never granted man dominion over his environment. The Greeks, who excelled in philosophical noesis, were less skillful in technological achievements. Modern science has emerged victorious from its encounter with nature because it has sacrificed qualitative-metaphysical speculation for the sake of a functional duplication of reality and substituted the *quantus* for the *qualis* question. Therefore, Adam the first is interested in just a single aspect of reality and asks one question only—"How does the cosmos function?" He is not fascinated by the question, "Why does the cosmos function at all?" nor is he interested in the question, "What is its essence?" He is only curious to know how it works. In fact, even this "how" question with which Adam the first is preoccupied is limited in scope. He is concerned not with the question *per se*, but with its practical implications. He raises not a metaphysical but a practical, technical "how" question. To be precise, his question is related not to the genuine functioning of the cosmos in itself but to the possibility of reproducing the dynamics of the cosmos by employing quantified-mathematized media which man evolves through postulation and creative thinking. The conative movement of attraction which Adam the first experiences toward the world is not of an exploratory-cognitive nature. It is rather nurtured by the selfish desire on the part of Adam to better his own position in relation to his environment. Adam the first is overwhelmed by one quest, namely, to harness and dominate the elemental natural forces and to put them at his disposal. This practical interest arouses his will to learn the secrets of nature. He is completely utilitarian as far as motivation, teleology, design, and methodology are concerned.

WHAT IS Adam the first out to achieve? What is the objective toward which he incessantly drives himself with enormous speed? The objective, it is self-evident, can be only one, namely, that which God put up before him: to be "man," to be himself. Adam the first wants to be human, to discover his identity which is bound up with his humanity. How does Adam find himself? He works with a simple equation introduced by the Psalmist, who proclaimed the singularity and unique station of man in nature: "For thou made him a little lower than the angels and hast crowned him with glory and honor (dignity)."* Man is an honorable being.

*As a matter of fact, the term *kavod* has a dual meaning in

In other words, man is a dignified being and to be human means to live with dignity. However, this equation of two unknown qualities requires further elaboration. We must be ready to answer the question: What is dignity and how can it be realized? The answer we find again in the words of the Psalmist, who addressed himself to this obvious question and who termed man not only an honorable but also a glorious being, spelling out the essence of glory in unmistakable terms: "Thou hast made him to have dominion over the works of Thy hands. Thou hast put all things under his feet." In other words, dignity was equated by the Psalmist with man's capability of dominating his environment and exercising control over it. Man acquires dignity through glory, through his *majestic* posture vis-à-vis his environment.*

---

Hebrew: (1) majesty, as in the phrase כבוד מלכותו; (2) dignity, as in the Halakhic phrase כבוד הבריות. That dignity is a criterion by which the worth of an individual is measured can be demonstrated by the halakhah that בזויים, self-abased persons, are disqualified from giving testimony. In particular, the phrase האוכל בשוק דומה לכלב, "whoever eats in the street or at any public place acts like a dog," used by both the Talmud (*Kiddushin* 40b) and Maimonides (*Mishneh Torah, Edut* XI, 5) is characteristic of the attitude of the Halakhah toward a man who has lost his sense of dignity. Likewise, I wish to point out the law that the principle of human dignity overrides certain Halakhic injunctions: vide *Berakhot* 19b. See also Nachmanides, Leviticus 19:1 (the description of the quality of sanctity).

*It might be pointed out that in the Septuagint the word כבוד is

---

15

The brute's existence is an undignified one because it is a helpless existence. Human existence is
a dignified one because it is a glorious, majestic,
powerful existence. Hence, dignity is unobtainable
as long as man has not reclaimed himself from
coexistence with nature and has not risen from a
non-reflective, degradingly helpless instinctive life
to an intelligent, planned, and majestic one. For
the sake of clarification of the double equation
humanity = dignity and dignity = glory-majesty,
it is necessary to add another thought. There is no
dignity without responsibility, and one cannot assume responsiblity as long as he is not capable of
living up to his commitments. Only when man
rises to the heights of freedom of action and creativity of mind does he begin to implement the
mandate of dignified responsibility entrusted to
him by his Maker. Dignity of man expressing itself
in the awareness of being responsible and of being
capable of discharging his responsibility cannot be
realized as long as he has not gained mastery over

---

here given an intellectualistic coloring, being rendered as *doxē*. The
Vulgate has the more literal *gloria*. In other contexts in which the
term כבוד signifies the human personality rather than honor, it is
variously translated. See, e.g., Psalms 16:9, לכן שמח לבי ויגל כבודי,
where כבודי is rendered *bē glossa mou* and *lingua mea*, respec-
tively; and Psalms 30:13, למען יזמרך כבוד, where כבוד is translated as
*bē doxa mou* and *gloria mea*.

his environment. For life in bondage to insensate elemental forces is a non-responsible and hence an undignified affair.*

Man of old who could not fight disease and succumbed in multitudes to yellow fever or any other plague with degrading helplessness could not lay claim to dignity. Only the man who builds hospitals, discovers therapeutic techniques, and saves lives is blessed with dignity. Man of the seventeenth and eighteenth centuries who needed several days to travel from Boston to New York was less dignified than modern man who attempts to conquer space, boards a plane at the New York airport at midnight and takes several hours later a leisurely walk along the streets of London.† The brute is helpless, and, therefore, not dignified. Civilized man has gained limited control of nature and has become, in certain respects, her master, and with his mastery he has attained dignity as well. His mastery has made it possible for him to act in accordance with his responsibility.

---

*Vide Nachmanides, Genesis 1:24: כדכתיב וכבוד והדר תעטרהו והוא מגמת פניו בחכמה וברעת וכשרון המעשה "As it is written, 'and (Thou) hast crowned him with honor and glory,' which refers to his (i.e., man's) intelligent, wise, and technically resourceful striving."

†It is obvious that this essay refers to Adam the first as a type representing the collective human technological genius, and not to individual members of the human race.

---

Hence, Adam the first is aggressive, bold, and victory-minded. His motto is success, triumph over the cosmic forces. He engages in creative work, trying to imitate his Maker (*imitatio Dei*). The most characteristic representative of Adam the first is the mathematical scientist who whisks us away from the array of tangible things, from color and sound, from heat, touch, and smell which are the only phenomena accessible to our senses, into a formal relational world of thought constructs, the product of his "arbitrary" postulating and spontaneous positing and deducing. This world, woven out of human thought processes, functions with amazing precision and runs parallel to the workings of the real multifarious world of our senses. The modern scientist does not try to explain nature. He only duplicates it. In his full resplendent glory as a creative agent of God, he constructs his own world and in mysterious fashion succeeds in controlling his environment through manipulating his own mathematical constructs and creations.

Adam the first is not only a creative theoretician. He is also a creative aesthete. He fashions ideas with his mind, and beauty with his heart. He enjoys both his intellectual and his aesthetic creativity and takes pride in it. He also displays creativity in the world of the norm: he legislates for himself norms and laws because a dignified existence is an orderly one. Anarchy and dignity are mutually exclusive. He is this-worldly-minded, finitude-oriented, beauty-centered. Adam the first is always an aesthete, whether engaged in an intellectual or in an ethical performance. His conscience is energized not by the idea of the good, but by that of the beautiful. His mind is questing not for the true, but for the pleasant and functional, which are rooted in the aesthetical, not the noetic-ethical, sphere.*

In doing all this, Adam the first is trying to carry out the mandate entrusted to him by his Maker who, at dawn of the sixth mysterious day of creation, addressed Himself to man and summoned him to "fill the earth and subdue it." It is God who decreed that the story of Adam the first be the great saga of freedom of man-slave who gradually transforms himself into man-master. While pursuing this goal, driven by an urge which he cannot but obey, Adam the first transcends the limits of the reasonable and probable and ventures into the open spaces of a boundless universe. Even this longing for vastness, no matter how adventurous

---

*It is worthwhile to note that Maimonides interpreted the story of the fall of man in terms of the betrayal of the intellectual and the ethical for the sake of the aesthetic. The Hebrew phrase עץ הדעת טוב ורע was translated by Maimonides as "And the tree of experiencing the pleasant and unpleasant."

and fantastic, is legitimate. Man reaching for the distant stars is acting in harmony with his nature which was created, willed, and directed by his Maker. It is a manifestation of obedience to rather than rebellion against God. Thus, in sum, we have obtained the following triple equation: humanity = dignity = responsibility = majesty.

# II

ADAM THE SECOND is, like Adam the first, also intrigued by the cosmos. Intellectual curiosity drives them both to confront courageously the *mysterium magnum* of Being. However, while the cosmos provokes Adam the first to quest for power and control, thus making him ask the functional "how" question, Adam the second responds to the call of the cosmos by engaging in a different kind of cognitive gesture. He does not ask a single functional question. Instead his inquiry is of a metaphysical nature and a threefold one. He wants to know: "Why is it?" "What is it?" "Who is it?" (1) He wonders: "Why did the world in its totality come into existence? Why is man confronted by this stupendous and indifferent order of things and events?" (2) He asks: "What is the purpose of all this? What is the message that is embedded in organic and inorganic matter, and what does the great challenge reaching me from beyond the fringes of the universe as well as from the depths of my tormented soul mean?" (3) Adam the second keeps on wondering: "Who is He who trails me steadily, uninvited and unwanted, like an everlasting shadow, and vanishes into the recesses of transcendence the very instant I turn around to confront this numinous, awesome, and mysterious 'He'? Who is He who fills Adam with awe and bliss, humility and a sense of greatness, concurrently? Who is He to whom Adam clings in passionate, all-consuming love and from whom he flees in mortal fear and dread? Who is He who fascinates Adam irresistibly and at the same time rejects him irrevocably? Who is He whom Adam experiences both as the *mysterium tremendum* and as the most elementary, most obvious, and most understandable truth? Who is He who is *deus revelatus* and *deus absconditus* simultaneously? Who is He whose life-giving and life-warming breath Adam feels constantly and who at the same time remains distant and remote from all?"

In order to answer this triple question, Adam the second does not apply the functional method invented by Adam the first. He does not create a world of his own. Instead, he wants to understand the living, "given" world into which he has been

cast. Therefore, he does not mathematize phenomena or conceptualize things. He encounters the
universe in all its colorfulness, splendor, and grandeur, and studies it with the naïveté, awe, and
admiration of the child who seeks the unusual and
wonderful in every ordinary thing and event. While
Adam the first is dynamic and creative, transforming sensory data into thought constructs, Adam
the second is receptive and beholds the world in its
original dimensions. He looks for the image of God
not in the mathematical formula or the natural
relational law but in every beam of light, in every
bud and blossom, in the morning breeze and the
stillness of a starlit evening. In a word, Adam the
second explores not the scientific abstract universe
but the irresistibly fascinating qualitative world
where he establishes an intimate relation with
God. The Biblical metaphor referring to God
breathing life into Adam alludes to the actual
preoccupation of the latter with God, to his genuine living experience of God rather than to some
divine potential or endowment in Adam symbolized by *imago Dei.** Adam the second lives in close

---

*Vide Nachmanides, Genesis 2:7: ויאמר כי הוא נפח באפיו נשמת חיים
להודיע כי לא באה בו מן היסודות ... גם לא בהשתלשלות מן השכלים הנבדלים אבל
היא רוח השם הגדול "And it is stated that He (i.e., God)
breathed into his (i.e., man's) nostrils the breath of life because it
(i.e., the soul) was not formed of the elements . . . nor did it
emanate from the Separate Intelligences but it was God's own
breath."

union with God. His existential "I" experience is interwoven in the awareness of communing with the Great Self whose footprints he discovers along the many tortuous paths of creation.

I STATED PREVIOUSLY that both Adams are equally provoked by the mystery of Being even though the methods they employ in their heroic attempt to come to terms and to arrange a *modus vivendi* with the *mysterium magnum* are incongruous. Let me add now that not only the etiological impulse and drive but also the objective and hence the motivation are identical. Both Adams want to be human. Both strive to be themselves, to be what God commanded them to be, namely, man. They certainly could not reach for some other objective since this urge, as I noted, lies, in accordance with God's scheme of creation, at the root of all human strivings and any rebellious effort on the part of man to substitute something else for this urge would be in distinct opposition to God's will which is embedded in man's nature. The incongruity of methods is, therefore, a result not of diverse objectives but of diverse interpretive approaches to the one objective they both pursue. The two Adams do not concur in their interpretations of this objective. The idea of humanity, the great challenge summoning man to action and movement, is placed by them in two incommensurate perspectives.

While Adam the first wants to reclaim himself from a closed-in, non-reflective, natural existence by setting himself up as a dignified majestic being capable of ruling his environment, Adam the second sees his *separateness* from nature and his existential uniqueness not in dignity or majesty but in something else. There is, in his opinion, another mode of existence through which man can find his own self, namely, the redemptive, which is not necessarily identical with the dignified. Quite often, an existence might be replete with dignity and mastery, and yet remain unredeemed. An atheist cosmonaut circling the earth, advising his superiors who placed him in orbit that he did not encounter any angels, might lay claim to dignity because he courageously mastered space; he is, however, very far from experiencing a redeemed existence.

In order to delineate more sharply the contours of Adam the second, who rejected dignity as the sole objective of human questing, let us add the following observation. Dignity is a social and behavioral category, expressing not an intrinsic existential quality but a technique of living, a way of impressing society, the knowhow of commanding respect and attention of the other fellow, a capacity to make one's presence felt. In Hebrew, the noun *kavod*, dignity, and the noun *koved*, weight, *gravitas*, stem from the same root. The man of dignity is a weighty person. The people who surround him feel his impact. Hence, dignity is measured not by the inner worth of the in-depth personality, but by the accomplishments of the surface personality. No matter how fine, noble, and gifted one may be, he cannot command respect or be appreciated by others if he has not succeeded in realizing his talents and communicating his message to society through the medium of the creative majestic gesture. In light of the aforementioned, dignity as a behavioral category can find realization only in the outward gesture which helps the inner personality to objectify itself and to explain and interpret itself to the external world. Hence, dignity can only be predicated of *kerygmatic* man, who has the capability of establishing lines of communication with neighbors, acquaintances, and friends, and of engaging them in a dialogue, not of words, but of action. Dignity is linked with fame. There is no dignity in anonymity. If one succeeds in putting his message (*kerygma*) across he may lay claim to dignity. The silent person, whose message remains hidden and suppressed in the in-depth personality, cannot be considered dignified.

Therefore, Adam the first was created not alone,

but together with Eve—male and female emerged simultaneously. Adam the first exists in society, in community with others. He is a social being, gregarious, communicative, emphasizing the artistic aspect in life and giving priority to form over content, to literary expression over the eidos, to practical accomplishments over inner motivation. He is blessed with the gift of rhetoric, with the faculty of communication, be it the beautiful word, the efficacious machine, the socially acceptable ethic-etiquette, or the hush of the solemn memorial assembly. The visible, perceptible public image of the personality is fraught with majesty and dignity. Adam the first is never alone. Man in solitude has no opportunity to display his dignity and majesty, since both are behavioral social traits. Adam the first was not left alone even on the day of creation. He emerged into the world together with Eve and God addressed himself to both of them as inseparable members of one community.

# III

THE COMMUNITY of which Adam the first, majestic man, is a member, is a natural one, a product of the creative, social gesture in which Adam engages whenever he thinks that collective living and acting will promote his interests.* I term this community a natural one, because the urge for organized activity at this level is not nurtured by the singular needs and experiences of spiritual man created in God's image

*The social-contract theory is not to be interpreted in chronological terms. It never claimed that individuals ever existed outside of society. The precedence of the individual over society is to be interpreted in conceptual terms: a Robinson Crusoe existence is thinkable and morally justified. The most important practical inference to be drawn from this theory is the moral right of the individual or individuals to secede from an existing society and form a new one. This kind of thinking, as we know, played an enormous role in the American as well as in the French Revolution. Therefore, there is no contradiction between the Biblical story of the creation of Adam the first and the social-contract theory.

but by biological, instinctual pressures. It is a natural reaction on the part of man, as a biological being bent on survival, to the menacing challenge of the outside world. In fact, the root of the instinct of gregariousness which is the very foundation of the natural community is to be found already in the animal kingdom. Let cattle grazing quietly along a wide area of green pastures sense suddenly that danger is lurking somewhere, they, overcome by instinctive panic, will begin to herd together and to cling to each other as if mere physical contiguity could avert the impending catastrophe. The difference between man associating with others and animals flocking together consists, of course, in the fact that while the mute creatures *react* in a mechanical, spurious, and purposeless way, eloquent and wise man *acts* intelligently and teleologically. Yet this discrepancy does not contradict our premise that the primordial urge to come together in face of opposition is shared by both animal and biological man.

Adam the first is challenged by a hostile environment and hence summoned to perform many tasks which he alone cannot master. Consequently, he is impelled to take joint action. Helpless individuals, cognizant of the difficulties they encounter when they act separately, congregate, make arrangements, enter into treaties of mutual assistance, sign contracts, form partnerships, etc.* The natural community is born of a feeling of individual helplessness. Whenever Adam the first wants to work, to produce, and to succeed in his undertakings, he must unite with others. The whole theory of the social contract, brought to perfection by the philosophers of the Age of Reason, reflects the thinking of Adam the first, identifying man with his intellectual nature and creative technological will and finding in human existence coherence, legitimacy, and reasonableness exclusively. To the thinkers of the Age of Reason man posed no problem. He was for them an understandable, simple affair. Their admiration, alas adoration, of the human mind hindered them from realizing the metaphysical dilemma and existential paradoxicality, indeed absurdity, embedded in the human "I" awareness. They saw man in his glory but failed to see him in his tragic plight. They considered the individual ontologically perfect and existentially adequate.† They admitted only that he was func-

*I am using the social-contract theory as an illustration of the functional character of the community formed by Adam the first. However, I could also demonstrate this idea by introducing organic theories of society which emphasize the primacy of society over the individual. Even, and perhaps primarily, the corporate state is of a functional character.

†The same naïveté in evaluating the role of man is to be found in the Marxist philosophical anthropology.

tionally handicapped even though he could, like Robinson Crusoe, surmount this difficulty, too. If the individual is ontologically complete, even perfect, then the experience of loneliness must be alien to him, since loneliness is nothing but the act of questioning one's own ontological legitimacy, worth, and reasonableness. In fact, according to the Biblical story, God was not concerned with the loneliness of Adam the first. Neither was Adam aware of the pronouncement לא טוב היות האדם לבדו, "It is not good for man to be lonely." Moreover, the connotation of these words in the context of the world view of Adam the first, even if they had been addressed to him, would have been related not to loneliness, an existential in-depth experience, but to aloneness, a practical surface experience. Adam the first, representing the natural community, would translate this pronouncement into pragmatic categories, referring not to existence as such, but to productive work. If pressed for an interpretation of the pronouncement, he would paraphrase it, "It is not good for man to work (not to be) alone," לא טוב עשות האדם מלאכה לבדו. The words "I shall make him a helpmate" would refer, in accordance with his social philosophy, to a functional partner to whom it would be assigned to collaborate with and assist Adam the first in his undertakings, schemes, and projects. Eve vis-à-vis

Adam the first would be a work partner, not an existential co-participant. Man alone cannot succeed, says Adam the first, because a successful life is possible only within a communal framework. Robinson Crusoe may be self-sufficient as far as mere survival is concerned, but he cannot make a success of his life. Distribution of labor, the coordinated efforts of the many, the accumulated experiences of the multitude, the cooperative spirit of countless individuals, raise man above the primitive level of a natural existence and grant him limited dominion over his environment. What we call civilization is the sum total of a community effort through the millennia. Thus, the natural community fashioned by Adam the first is a work community, committed to the successful production, distribution, and consumption of goods, material as well as cultural.

Ecclesiastes (Kohelet) has portrayed the act of grouping and coalescing as envisioned by Adam the first in unmistakable categories: "The two are better than the one because they have a good reward for their labor. For if they fall, the one will lift up his fellow; but woe to him that is alone when he falleth, and hath not another to help him out." The natural community of Adam the first enhances man's chances for successful survival, yet does not elevate or enhance his existential experience, since the latter is in no need of redemption or catharsis. Adam the first feels safer and more comfortable in the company of Eve in a practical, not ontological, way. He will never admit that he cannot, ontologically, see himself without Eve. They, Adam and Eve, act together, work together, pursue common objectives together; yet they do not exist together. Ontologically, they do not belong to each other; each is provided with an "I" awareness and knows nothing of a "We" awareness. Of course, they communicate with each other. But the communication lines are open between two surface personalities engaged in work, dedicated to success, and speaking in clichés and stereotypes, and not between two souls bound together in an indissoluble relation, each one speaking in unique *logoi*. The in-depth personalities do not communicate, let alone commune, with each other. "And God blessed them and God said unto them be fruitful and multiply and replenish the earth and subdue it and have dominion over the fish of the sea, and over the fowl of the air, and over everything that creepeth over the earth."

Male and female were summoned by their creator to act in unison in order to act successfully. Yet they were not charged with the task of existing in unison, in order to cleanse, redeem, and hallow their existence.

# IV

HAVING DESCRIBED majestic Adam both as an individual and as a member of a work community, let us return to Adam the second in his dual role as a lonely individual and as one committed to a peculiar community idea.

There are two basic distinctions between dignity and cathartic redemptiveness:

1. Being redeemed is, unlike being dignified, an ontological awareness. It is not just an extraneous, accidental attribute—among other attributes—of being, but a definitive mode of being itself. A redeemed existence is intrinsically different from an unredeemed. Redemptiveness does not have to be acted out vis-à-vis the outside world.* Even a

---

*The Halakhic requirement of dignified behavior, כבוד הבריות,

hermit, while not having the opportunity to manifest dignity, can live a redeemed life. Cathartic redemptiveness is experienced in the privacy of one's in-depth personality, and it cuts below the relationship between the "I" and the "thou" (to use an existentialist term) and reaches into the very hidden strata of the isolated "I" who knows himself as a singular being. When objectified in personal and emotional categories, cathartic redemptiveness expresses itself in the feeling of axiological security. The individual intuits his existence as worthwhile, legitimate, and adequate, anchored in something stable and unchangeable.

2. Cathartic redemptiveness, in contrast to dignity, cannot be attained through man's acquisition of control of his environment, but through man's exercise of control over himself. A redeemed life is *ipso facto* a disciplined life. While a dignified exis-

---

applies in some cases to public actions while in other cases even to one's private actions. The problem of כבוד הבריות with which the Talmud, *Berakhot* 19b, deals is related to public offensive actions, such as disrobing, while in *Shabbat* 81a and *Eruvin* 41b, the Talmud is concerned with undignified action even in private. Apparently, the determining factor in these cases is the nature of the act itself. A certain act, such as disrobing, is unworthy only if exposed to public view, whereas another, such as the lack of bodily hygiene, is always disgraceful. This Halakhic approach does not contradict our viewpoint that dignity is a social behavioral category and that the hermit cannot realize it in full.

tence is attained by majestic man who courageously surges forward and confronts mute nature—a lower form of being—in a mood of
defiance, redemption is achieved when humble
man makes a movement of recoil, and lets himself
be confronted and defeated by a Higher and Truer
Being. God summoned Adam the first to advance
steadily, Adam the second to retreat. Adam the
first He told to exercise mastery and to "fill the
earth and subdue it," Adam the second, to serve.
He was placed in the Garden of Eden "to cultivate
it and to keep it."

Dignity is acquired by man whenever he triumphs over nature. Man finds redemption whenever he is overpowered by the Creator of nature.
Dignity is discovered at the summit of success;
redemption in the depth of crisis and failure: ממעמקים
קראתיך ה', "Out of the depths have I called thee, O
God." The Bible has stated explicitly that Adam
the second was formed from the dust of the ground
because the knowledge of the humble origin of
man is an integral part of Adam's "I" experience.
Adam the second has never forgotten that he is just
a handful of dust.*

*The Halakhah has linked human distress with the human capa-
bility of renewal and self-transformation. Man's confrontation with
evil and suffering must result, according to the Halakhah, in the
great act of *teshuvah* (repentance). "In thy distress when all these
things are come upon thee . . . thou wilt return to the Lord thy
God and hearken unto His voice" (Deut. 4:30).

AND DEFEATED must Adam the second feel the very instant he scores his greatest success: the discovery of his humanity, his "I" identity. The "I" awareness which he attains as the result of his untiring search for a redeemed, secure existence brings its own antithesis to the fore: the awareness of his exclusiveness and ontological incompatibility with any other being. Adam the second suddenly finds out that he is alone, that he has alienated himself from the world of the brute and the instinctual mechanical state of an outward existence, while he has failed to ally himself with the intelligent, purposive inward beings who inhabit the new world into which he has entered. Each great redemptive step forward in man's quest for humanity entails the ever-growing tragic awareness of his aloneness and only-ness and consequently of his loneliness and insecurity. He struggles for the discovery of his identity because he suffers from the insecurity implied in seeing the icy darkness of uniformity and irresponsiveness, in gazing into that senseless something without being awarded a reciprocal gaze, in being always a silent watcher without in turn being watched. With the redeeming daybreak of a new "I" identity, Adam the second is ushered into a world of diversity and change where the feeling of insecurity expresses itself in the fact that the term "man" clothes a wondrous, unique, and incommunicable reality, in the gazing into somebody who returns one's gaze suspiciously, in watching and being watched in bewilderment. Who knows what kind of loneliness is more agonizing: the one which befalls man when he casts his glance at the mute cosmos, at its dark spaces and monotonous drama, or the one that besets man exchanging glances with his fellow man in silence? Who knows whether the first astronaut who will land on the moon, confronted with a strange, weird, and grisly panorama, will feel a greater loneliness than Mr. X, moving along jubilantly with the crowd and exchanging greetings on New Year's Eve at a public square?

Adam the second is still lonely. He separated himself from his environment which became the object of his intellectual gaze. "And the man gave names to all the beasts and to the fowl of the heaven and to every animal of the field." He is a citizen of a new world, the world of man, but he has no companion with whom to communicate and therefore he is existentially insecure. Neither would the availability of the female, who was created with Adam the first, have changed this human situation if not for the emergence of a new kind of companionship. At this crucial point, if Adam is to bring his quest for redemption to full realization, he must initiate action leading to the discovery of a companion who, even though as unique and singular as he, will master the art of communicating and, with him, form a community. However, this action, since it is part of the redemptive gesture, must also be sacrificial. The medium of attaining full redemption is, again, defeat. This new companionship is not attained through conquest, but through surrender and retreat. "And the eternal God caused an overpowering sleep to fall upon the man." Adam was overpowered and defeated—and in defeat he found his companion.

Again, the contrast between the two Adams comes into focus. Adam the first was not called to sacrifice in order that his female companion come into being, while it was indispensable for Adam the second to give away part of himself in order to find a companion. The community-fashioning gesture of Adam the first is, as I indicated before, purely utilitarian and intrinsically egotistic and, as such, rules out sacrificial action. For Adam the second, communicating and communing are redemptive sacrificial gestures. Thus, in crisis and distress there was planted the seed of a new type of community—the faith community which reached full fruition in the covenant between God and Abraham.*

*The Biblical account of the original sin is the story of man of

THE COVENANTAL faith community, in contradistinction to the natural work community, interprets the divine pronouncement "It is not
good for man to be alone," לא טוב היות האדם לבדו, not
in utilitarian but in ontological terms: it is not good
for man to be lonely (not alone) with emphasis
placed upon "to be." Being at the level of the faith
community does not lend itself to any equation.
"To be" is not to be equated with "to work and
produce goods" (as historical materialism wants us
to believe). "To be" is not identical with "to think"
(as the classical tradition of philosophical rational-
ism throughout the ages, culminating in Descartes
and later in Kant, tried to convince us). "To be"
does not exhaust itself either in suffering (as Scho-
penhauer preached) or in enjoying the world of
sense (in accordance with ethical hedonism). "To
be" is a unique in-depth experience of which only
Adam the second is aware, and it is unrelated to
any function or performance. "To be" means to be

---

faith who realizes suddenly that faith can be utilized for the
acquisition of majesty and glory and who, instead of fostering a
covenantal community, prefers to organize a political utilitarian
community exploiting the sincerity and unqualified commitment of
the crowd for non-covenantal, worldly purposes. The history of
organized religion is replete with instances of desecration of the
covenant.

the only one, singular and different, and consequently lonely. For what causes man to be lonely and feel insecure if not the awareness of his uniqueness and exclusiveness? The "I" is lonely, experiencing ontological incompleteness and casualness, because there is no one who exists like the "I" and because the *modus existentiae* of the "I" cannot be repeated, imitated, or experienced by others.

Since loneliness reflects the very core of the "I" experience and is not an accidental *modus*, no accidental activity or external achievement—such as belonging to a natural work community and achieving cooperative success—can reclaim Adam the second from this state. Therefore, I repeat, Adam the second must quest for a different kind of community. The companionship which Adam the second is seeking is not to be found in the depersonalized regimentation of the army, in the automatic coordination of the assembly line, or in the activity of the institutionalized, soulless political community. His quest is for a new kind of fellowship, which one finds in the existential community. There, not only hands are joined, but experiences as well; there, one hears not only the rhythmic sound of the production line, but also the rhythmic beat of hearts starved for existential companionship and all-embracing sympathy and

experiencing the grandeur of the faith commitment; there, one lonely soul finds another soul
tormented by loneliness and solitude yet unqualifiedly committed.

# V

A T THIS POINT, the main distinction between the natural community of Adam the
first and the covenantal faith community of
Adam the second becomes clear. The first is a
community of interests, forged by the indomitable
desire for success and triumph and consisting at all
times of two grammatical *personae*, the "I" and the
"thou" who collaborate in order to further their
interests. A newcomer, upon joining the community, ceases to be the anonymous "he" and turns
into a knowable, communicative "thou." The second is a community of commitments born in distress and defeat and comprises three participants:
"I, thou, and He," the He in whom all being is
rooted and in whom everything finds its rehabili-
tation and, consequently, redemption. Adam the
first met the female all by himself, while Adam the

second was introduced to Eve by God, who summoned Adam to join Eve in an existential community molded by sacrificial action and suffering, and
who Himself became a partner in this community.
God is never outside the covenantal community.
He joins man and shares in his covenantal existence. Finitude and infinity, temporality and eternity, creature and creator become involved in the
same community. They bind themselves together
and participate in a unitive existence.*

The element of togetherness of God and man is
indispensable for the covenantal community, for
the very validity of the covenant rests upon the
juridic-Halakhic principle of free negotiation, mutual assumption of duties, and full recognition of
the equal rights of both parties concerned with the
covenant.[1] Both parties entering a covenantal relationship possess inalienable rights which may only
be surrendered by mutual consent. The paradoxical experience of freedom, reciprocity, and "equal-
ity" in one's personal confrontation with God is
basic for the understanding of the covenantal faith

*The whole concept of עמו אנכי בצרה "I shall be with him in
trouble" can only be understood within the perspective of the
covenantal community which involves God in the destiny of His
fellow members. Vide *Sanhedrin*, 46a; *Yerushalmi*, *Sukkah*, 4, 3.

44

community.* We meet God in the covenantal community as a comrade and fellow member. Of course, even within the framework of this community, God appears as the leader, teacher, and shepherd. Yet the leader is an integral part of the community, the teacher is inseparable from his pupils, and the shepherd never leaves his flock. They all belong to one group. The covenant draws God into the society of men of faith: "The God before whom my fathers did walk—the God who has been my shepherd all my life." God was Jacob's shepherd and companion. The covenantal faith community manifests itself in a threefold personal union: I, thou and He.†

*The strange Aggadic stories about a theoretical Halakhic "controversy" between the Almighty and the Heavenly Academy (מתיבתא דרקיעא) and about R. Joshua b. Chanania's rejecting a Divine decision which favored a minority opinion over that of the majority are characteristic of the intimate Halakhic-covenantal relationship prevailing between man and God. Vide *Bava Mezia* 59b and 86a.

†Vide Leviticus 26:12, *Sifra* and Rashi.

1. The giving of the law on Mount Sinai was a result of free negotiation between Moses and the people who consented to submit themselves to the Divine Will. The Halakhah treats the Sinai and Moab covenants in categories and terms governing any civil agreement. The Talmudic opinion (*Shabbat* 88a), כפה עליהם הר כגיגית, that there was coercive action on the part of God during the Sinai revelation, does not refute our thesis. The action to which the Talmud refers was taken after the covenant had been voluntarily

transacted on the preceding day (the fifth of Sivan) according to the chronology elaborated by Rashi (based on the *Mekhilta*). Even Nachmanides, who disagreed with Rashi and accepted the opposite view to the *Mekhilta*, placing the transaction on the seventh of Sivan after the ultimatum had been issued to the community, must admit that the latter obligated itself to abide by God's will prior to the revelation, as it is distinctly stated in Exodus 19:8. Nachmanides differs with Rashi only with reference to the solemn formalization of the covenant as told in Exodus 24:3–8.

In light of this, the Talmudic saying (*loc. cit.*) מכאן מודעה רבה לאורייתא is puzzling inasmuch as coercion was applied only to the implementation and not to the assumption of the covenantal obligation. To be sure, this phrase is not to be construed in its literal meaning, since no scholar has ever questioned the validity of the Sinai covenant even prior to its reaffirmation in the days of Mordecai and the other men of the Great Assembly to which the Talmud (*loc. cit.*) refers. The idea underlying this phrase is to be understood as referring to a moral mitigating circumstance rather than a juridic-Halakhic defense. See *Chiddushei ha-Ramban*, *ad locum*.

It appears that God required two commitments on the part of the community: a general one to abide by the will of God while the community was still unaware of the nature of the commitment and a specific one concerning each individual law. The second commitment was assumed under constraint. Vide *Mekhilta* quoted by Rashi, Exodus 20:1; Rashi and Nachmanides, Exodus, 24:1. *See Tosafot*, *Shabbat* 88a, sub מודעא, and *Kiddushin*, 61b.

The reason for introducing an element of coercion into the great Sinai covenant, in contradistinction, *prima facie*, to the Biblical story, lies in the idea that covenantal man feels overpowered and defeated by God even when he appears to be a free agent of his own will.

# VI

EVEN THOUGH, as we said before, the man of faith is provoked, like Adam the first, by the cosmos about which he is inquisitive, the covenant, not the cosmos, provides him with an answer to his questions. The covenantal confrontation is indispensable for the man of faith. In his longing for God, he is many a time disenchanted with the cosmic revelation and lives through moments of despair. Naturally, he is inspired by the great joy experienced when he gets a glimpse of the Truly Real hiding behind the magnificent cosmic facade. However, he is also tormented by the stress and exasperation felt when the Truly Real seems to disappear from the cosmic scene. Of course, God speaks through His works: השמים מספרים כבוד א־ל וגו׳, "The heavens declare the glory of God and the firmament showeth His handiwork." Yet, let me ask, what kind of a tale do the heavens tell? Is it a personal tale addressed to someone, or is it a tale which is not intended for any audience? Do the heavens sing the glory of the Creator without troubling themselves to find out whether someone is listening to this great song, or are they really interested in man, the listener? I believe that the answer to this question is obvious. If the tale of the heavens were a personal one, addressed to man, then there would be no need for another encounter with God. Since God in His infinite wisdom arranged for the apocalyptic-covenantal meeting with man, we may conclude that the message of the heavens is at best an equivocal one.

As a matter of fact, at the level of his cosmic confrontation with God, man is faced with an exasperating paradox. On the one hand, he beholds God in every nook and corner of creation, in the flowering of the plant, in the rushing of the tide, and in the movement of his own muscle, as if God were at hand close to and beside man, engaging him in a friendly dialogue. And yet the very moment man turns his face to God, he finds Him remote, unapproachable, enveloped in transcendence and mystery. Did not Isaiah behold God רם ונשא, exalted and enthroned above creation, and at the same time ושוליו מלאים את ההיכל, the train of his skirts filling the Temple, the great universe, from the flying nebulae to one's most intimate heartbeat? Did not the angels sing קדוש קדוש קדוש, holy, holy, holy, transcendent, transcendent, transcendent, yet ה׳ צב׳ מלא כל הארץ כבודו, He is the Lord of the hosts, who resides in every infinitesimal particle of creation and the whole universe is replete with His glory? In short, the cosmic experience is antithetic and tantalizing. It exhausts itself in the awesome dichotomy of God's involvement in the drama of creation, and His exaltedness above and remoteness from this very drama. This dichotomy cancels the intimacy and immediacy from one's relationship with God and renders the personal approach to God complicated and difficult. God, as the cosmic ruler, is beheld in His boundless majesty reigning supreme over creation, His will crystallized in the natural law, His word determining the behavioral patterns of nature. He is everywhere but at the same time above and outside of everything. When man who just beheld God's presence turns around to address himself to the Master of creation in the intimate accents of the "Thou," he finds the Master and Creator gone, enveloped in the cloud of mystery, winking to him from the awesome "beyond." Therefore, the man of faith, in order to redeem himself from his loneliness and misery, must meet God at a personal covenantal level, where he can be near Him and feel free in His presence. Abraham, the knight of faith, according to our tradition, sought and discovered God in the starlit heavens of Mesopotamia. Yet, he felt an intense loneliness and could not find solace in the silent companionship of God, whose image was reflected in the boundless stretches of the cosmos. Only when he met God on earth as Father, Brother, and Friend—not only along the uncharted astral routes—did he feel redeemed. Our sages said that before Abraham appeared *majestas dei* was reflected only by the distant heavens, and it was a mute nature which "spoke" of the glory of God. It was Abraham who "crowned" Him the God of earth, i.e., the God of men.[1]

Majestic man, even when he belongs to the group of *homines religiosi* and feels a distinct need for transcendental experiences, is gratified by his encounter with God within the framework of the cosmic drama. Since majestic man is incapable of breaking out of the cosmic cycle, he cannot interpret his transcendental adventure in anything but cosmic categories. Therefore, the divine name of E-lohim, which denotes God being the source of the cosmic dynamics, sufficed to characterize the relationship prevailing between majestic man and his Creator addressing Himself to him through the cosmic occurrence.

However, covenantal man of faith, craving for a personal and intimate relation with God, could not find it in the cosmic E-lohim encounter and had to shift his transcendental experience to a different level at which the finite "I" meets the infinite He "face-to-face." This strange communal relation between man and God is symbolized by the Tetragrammaton,* which therefore appears in the Biblical account of Adam the second.

*This distinction between E-lohim and the Tetragrammaton was developed in detail by Judah Halevi.

1. *Bereshit Rabbah*, 59; Rashi, Genesis 24:7. I intentionally used the term "cosmic" instead of "cosmological." While one may speak of the cosmic confrontation of man and God as an experiential reality, it is hard to speak of a cosmological experience. When God is apprehended *in* reality it is an experience; when God is comprehended *through* reality it is just an intellectual performance. Therefore, one must not equate the cosmic experience, no matter how inadequate it is, with Judah Halevi's "God of Aristotle." As we mentioned in the text, the cosmic experience is part of the patriarchial tradition. The Halakhah has granted full recognition to this experience, which is reflected in many of our benedictions.

The trouble with all rational demonstrations of the existence of God, with which the history of philosophy abounds, consists in their being exactly what they were meant to be by those who formulated them: abstract logical demonstrations divorced from the living primal experiences in which these demonstrations are rooted. For instance, the cosmic experience was transformed into a cosmological proof, the ontic experience into an ontological proof, et cetera. Instead of stating that the most elementary existential awareness as a subjective "I exist" and an objective "the world around me exists" awareness is unattainable as long as the ultimate reality of God is not part of this awareness, the theologians engaged in formal postulating and deducing in an experiential vacuum. Because of this, they exposed themselves to Hume's and Kant's biting criticism that logical categories are applicable only within the limits of the human scientific experience.

Does the loving bride in the embrace of her beloved ask for proof that he is alive and real? Must the prayerful soul clinging in passionate love and ecstasy to her Beloved demonstrate that He exists? So asked Soren Kierkegaard sarcastically when told that Anselm of Canterbury, the father of the very abstract and complex ontological proof, spent many days in prayer and supplication that he be presented with rational evidence of the existence of God.

Maimonides' term לידע (*Yesode ha-Torah*, 1:1) transcends the bounds of the abstract *logos* and passes over into the realm of the boundless intimate and impassioned experience where postulate and deduction, discursive knowledge and intuitive thinking, conception and perception, subject and object, are one. Only in paragraph five, after the aboriginal experience of God had been established by him as a firm reality (in paragraph one), does he introduce the Aristotelian cosmological proof of the unmoved mover.

# VII

I MENTIONED PREVIOUSLY that only the covenantal community consisting of all three grammatical *personae*—I, thou, and He—can and does alleviate the passional experience of Adam the second by offering him the opportunity to communicate, indeed to commune with, and to enjoy the genuine friendship of Eve. Within the covenantal community, I said, Adam and Eve participate in the existential experience of being, not merely working, together. The change from a technical utilitarian relationship to a covenantal existential one occurs in the following manner. When God joins the community of man the miracle of revelation takes place in two dimensions: in the transcendental—*Deus absconditus* emerges suddenly as *Deus revelatus*—and in the human—*homo absconditus* sheds his mask and turns into *homo revelatus*.

With the sound of the divine voice addressing man by his name, be it Abraham, Moses, or Samuel, God, whom man has sought along the endless trails of the universe, is discovered suddenly as being close to and intimate with man, standing just opposite or beside him. At this meeting—initiated by God—of God and man, the covenantal-prophetic community is established. When man addresses himself to God, calling Him in the informal, friendly tones of "Thou," the same miracle happens again: God joins man and at this meeting, initiated by man, a new covenantal community is born—the prayer community.

I have termed both communities, the prophetic and the prayerful, covenantal because of a threefold reason. (1) In both communities, a confrontation of God and man takes place. It is quite obvious that the prophecy awareness, which is *toto genere* different from the mystical experience, can only be interpreted in the unique categories of the covenantal event. The whole idea of prophecy would be fraught with an inner contradiction if man's approach to God remained indirect and impersonal, expecting nature to mediate between him and his Creator. Only within the covenantal community, which is formed by God descending upon the mount* and man, upon the call of the Lord,

---

*וירד ה׳ על הר סיני: "And the Lord came down upon Mount Sinai."

---

ascending the mount,* is a direct and personal relationship expressing itself in the prophetic "face-to-face" colloquy established. "And the Lord spake unto Moses face to face as man speaketh unto his friend."†

Prayer likewise is unimaginable without having man stand before and address himself to God in a manner reminiscent of the prophet's dialogue with God. The cosmic drama, notwithstanding its grandeur and splendor, no matter how distinctly it reflects the image of the Creator and no matter how beautifully it tells His glory, cannot provoke man to prayer. Of course, it may arouse an adoring-ecstatic mood in man; it may even inspire man to raise his voice in a song of praise and thanksgiving. Nevertheless, ecstatic adoration, even if expressed in a hymn, is not prayer. The latter transcends the bounds of liturgical worship and must not be reduced to its external-technical aspects such as praise, thanksgiving, or even petition.

---

*ויקרא ה׳ למשה אל ראש ההר ויעל משה: "And the Lord called Moses up to the top of the mount, and Moses went up."

†This verse telling us about the prophetic encounter of Moses with God describes the ideal state of prophecy as it was attained by Moses. The Bible itself in another passage contrasts the Mosaic confrontation with God with that of other prophets who failed to reach the same heights and hence experienced the numinous apocalyptic dread and awe. Vide Exodus 33:17; Numbers 12:6, 8; *Yesode ha-Torah*, VII: 6.

---

Prayer is basically an awareness of man finding himself in the presence of and addressing himself to his Maker, and to pray has one connotation only: to stand before God.* To be sure, this awareness has been objectified and crystallized in standardized, definitive texts whose recitation is obligatory. The total faith commitment tends always to transcend the frontiers of fleeting, amorphous subjectivity and to venture into the outside world of the well-formed, objective gesture. However, no matter how important this tendency on the part of the faith commitment is—and it is of enormous significance in the Halakhah, which constantly demands from man that he translate his inner life into external facticity—it remains unalterably true that the very essence of prayer is the covenantal experience of being together with and talking to God and that the concrete performance such as the recita-

---

*The fact that we commence the recital of the "Eighteen Benedictions" by addressing ourselves to the God of Abraham, Isaac, and Jacob is indicative of the covenantal relationship which, in the opinion of our sages, lies at the very root of prayer. The fact that prayer is founded upon the covenantal relationship is responsible for the omission of *Malkhut* (God's cosmic kinship or sovereignty) from the "Eighteen Benedictions." In order to avoid misunderstanding, I wish to add that the phrase *melekh ha-olam* (King of the universe) was eliminated from the basic benediction formula, while the term *melekh* (King) does appear in several places; vide Tosafot, *Berakhot* 40b sub אמר.

tion of texts represents the technique of implementation of prayer and not prayer itself.[1] In short, prayer and prophecy are two synonymous designations of the covenantal God–man colloquy. Indeed, the prayer community was born the very instant the prophetic community expired and, when it did come into the spiritual world of the Jew of old, it did not supersede the prophetic community but rather perpetuated it. Prayer is the continuation of prophecy, and the fellowship of prayerful men is *ipso facto* the fellowship of prophets. The difference between prayer and prophecy is, as I have already mentioned, related not to the substance of the dialogue but rather to the order in which it is conducted. While within the prophetic community God takes the initiative—He speaks and man listens—in the prayer community the initiative belongs to man: he does the speaking and God, the listening. The word of prophecy is God's and is accepted by man. The word of prayer is man's and God accepts it. The two Halakhic traditions tracing the origin of prayer to Abraham and the other Patriarchs and attributing the authorship of statutory prayer to the men of the Great Assembly reveal the Judaic view of the sameness of the prophecy and prayer communities.* Cove-

---

*Vide *Berakhot* 26b, 33a; *Megillah* 18a. It is not my intention here

nantal prophecy and prayer blossomed forth the very instant Abraham met God and became involved in a strange colloquy. At a later date, when the mysterious men of this wondrous assembly witnessed the bright summer day of the prophetic community, full of color and sound, turning to a bleak autumnal night of dreadful silence unillumined by the vision of God or made homely by His voice, they refused to acquiesce in this cruel historical reality and would not let the ancient dialogue between God and men come to an end. For the men of the Great Assembly knew that with the withdrawal of the colloquy from the field of consciousness of the Judaic community, the latter would lose the intimate companionship of God and consequently its covenantal status. In prayer they found the salvation of the colloquy, which, they insisted, must go on forever. If God had stopped calling man, they urged, let man call God. And so the covenantal colloquy was shifted from the level of prophecy to that of prayer.

(2) Both the prophetic and the prayerful communities are threefold structures, consisting of all three grammatical personae—I, thou, and He. The

---

to investigate the controversy between Maimonides and Nachmanides as to whether the precept of prayer is of Pentateuchic or Rabbinic origin. All agree that statutory standardized prayer was introduced by the men of the Great Assembly.

---

prophet in whom God confides and to whom He entrusts His eternal word must always remember that he is the representative of the many anonymous "they" for whom the message is earmarked. No man, however great and noble, is worthy of God's word if he fancies that the word is his private property not to be shared by others.*

The prayerful community must not, likewise, remain a twofold affair: a transient "I" addressing himself to the eternal "He." The inclusion of others is indispensable. Man should avoid praying for himself alone. The plural form of prayer is of central Halakhic significance.† When disaster strikes, one must not be immersed completely in his own passional destiny, thinking exclusively of himself, being concerned only with himself, and petitioning God merely for himself. The foundation of efficacious and noble prayer is human solidarity and sympathy or the covenantal awareness of existential togetherness, of sharing and experiencing the travail and suffering of those for whom

*The strict Halakhic censure of the prophet who fails to deliver the divine message underscores the public character of prophecy. Vide *Sanhedrin* 89a. It should be noted that Maimonides speaks also of prophecy confined to the individual; see *Yesode ha-Torah*, VII, 7 and *Moreh Nevukhim*, II, 37. However, such individual illumination cannot be termed covenantal prophecy.

†*Vide Berakhot* 12b; *Bava Kamma* 92a; *Shabbat* 12b.

majestic Adam the first has no concern. Only Adam the second knows the art of praying since he confronts God with the petition of the many. The fenced-in egocentric and ego-oriented Adam the first is ineligible to join the covenantal prayer community of which God is a fellow member. If God abandons His transcendental numinous solitude, He wills man to do likewise and to step out of his isolation and aloneness.* Job did not understand this simple postulate. "And it was so, when the days of their feasting were gone about, that Job sent and sanctified them, and rose up early in the morning, and offered burnt offerings according to the *"number of them all.*"† He did pray, he did offer sacrifices, but only for his household. Job failed to understand the covenantal nature of the prayer community in which destinies are dovetailed, suffering or joy is shared, and prayers merge into one petition on behalf of all. As we all know, Job's sacrifices were not accepted, Job's prayers remained unheard, and Job—pragmatic Adam the first—met with catastrophe and the whirlwind uprooted him and his household. Only then did he discover the great covenantal experience of being

---

*This is the reason underlying the institution of תפלת הציבור, the recital of prayers with the congregation, which occupies such a prominent position in the Halakhah.

†Job 1:5. See *Bava Kamma* 92a.

---

together, praying together and for one another. "And the Lord turned the captivity of Job, when he prayed for his friends; also the Lord gave Job twice as much as he had before." Not only was Job rewarded with a double measure in material goods, but he also attained a new dimension of existence— the covenantal one.

(3) Both communities sprang into existence not only because of a singular experience of having met God, but also and perhaps mainly because of the discovery of the normative *kerygma* entailed in this very experience. Any encounter with God, if it is to redeem man, must be crystallized and objectified in a normative ethico-moral message. If, however, the encounter is reduced to its non-kerygmatic and non-imperative aspects, no matter how great and magnificent an experience it is, it cannot be classified as a covenantal encounter since the very semantics of the term "covenant" implies freely assumed obligations and commitments. In contradistinction to the mystical experience of intuition, illumination, or union which rarely results in the formulation of a practical message, prophecy, which, as I emphasized before, has very little in common with the mystical experience, is inseparable from its normative content. Isaiah, Ezekiel, or other prophets were not led through the habitations of heaven, past the seraphim and angels, to

the hidden recesses where God is enthroned above
and beyond everything in order to get the overpowering glimpse of the Absolute, True, and Real, and
to bring their individual lives to complete fulfillment. The prophetic pilgrimage to God pursues a
practical goal in whose realization the whole covenantal community shares. When confronted with
God, the prophet receives an ethico-moral message
to be handed down to and realized by the members
of the covenantal community, which is mainly a
community in action. What did Isaiah hear when
he beheld God sitting on the throne, high and
exalted? "Also I heard the voice of the Lord saying,
'Whom shall I send and who will go for us . . . ?' "
What did Ezekiel hear when he completed his
journey through the heavenly hierarchy to the
mysterious sanctuary of God? "And He said unto
me: son of man, I send thee to the children of
Israel, to a rebellious nation that hath rebelled
against me. . . ." The prophet is a messenger
carrying the great divine imperative addressed to
the covenantal community. "So I turned and came
down from the mount. . . . And the two tablets of
the covenant were on my two hands." This terse
description by Moses of his noble role as the carrier
of the two tablets of stone on which the divine
norm was engraved has universal significance appli-

cable to all prophets.* "I will raise them up a prophet . . . and will put my words into his mouth. . . . Whosoever will not hear unto my words which he shall speak in my name, I will require of him."

The above-said, which is true of the universal faith community in general, has particular validity for the Halakhic community. The prime purpose of revelation in the opinion of the Halakhah is related to the giving of the Law. The God–man confrontation serves a didactic goal. God involves Himself in the covenantal community through the medium of teaching and instructing. The Halakhah has looked upon God since time immemorial as the teacher par excellence.† This educational task was in turn entrusted to the prophet whose greatest ambition is to teach the covenantal com-

---

*That every prophecy is normative does not contradict the statement of our sages, אלה המצות שאין נביא רשאי לחדש דבר מעתה, that no prophet is allowed to change even the smallest detail of the law (*Torat Kohanim* 120; *Temurah* 16a; *Shabbat* 104a; *Megillah* 3a; *Yoma* 80a). The adjective "normative" has a dual connotation: first, legislative action; second, exhortatory action. While Moses' prophecy established a new covenant entailing a new moral code, the prophecies of his followers addressed themselves to the commitment taken on by the covenantal community to realize the covenant in full. Vide *Chagigah* 10b; *Bava Kamma* 2b; *Niddah* 23a; *Yesode ha-Torah* IX, 1–4.

†There are many allusions in our Aggadah and liturgy to the teaching of Torah as part of God's "routine."

munity. In short, God's word is *ipso facto* God's law and norm.

Let me add that for Judaism the reverse would be not only unthinkable but immoral as well. If we were to eliminate the norm from the prophetic God–man encounter, confining the latter to its apocalyptic aspects, then the whole prophetic drama would be acted out by a limited number of privileged individuals to the exclusion of the rest of the people.* Such a prospect, turning the prophetic colloquy into an esoteric-egotistic affair, would be immoral from the viewpoint of Halakhic Judaism, which is exoterically-minded and democratic to its very core. The democratization of the God–man confrontation was made possible by the centrality of the normative element in prophecy. Only the norm engraved upon the two tablets of stone, visible and accessible to all, draws the people into this confrontation "Ye are placed this day, all of you, before the Eternal, your God; your heads of your tribes, your elders and your bailiffs, with all the men of Israel . . . from the hewer of thy wood unto the drawer of thy water." And how can the woodchopper and the water drawer participate in this adventurous meeting of God and man, if

---

*According to our tradition, the entire community, even at the revelation at Sinai, heard only the first two, not all ten, commandments. Vide *Makkot* 24a.

not through helping in a humble way to realize the covenantal norm?

Prayer likewise consists not only of an awareness of the presence of God, but of an act of committing oneself to God and accepting His ethico-moral authority.[2]

Who is qualified to engage God in the prayer colloquy? Clearly, the person who is ready to cleanse himself of imperfection and evil. Any kind of injustice, corruption, cruelty, or the like desecrates the very essence of the prayer adventure, since it encases man in an ugly little world into which God is unwilling to enter. If man craves to meet God in prayer, then he must purge himself of all that separates him from God. The Halakhah has never looked upon prayer as a separate magical gesture in which man may engage without integrating it into the total pattern of his life. God hearkens to prayer if it rises from a heart contrite over a muddled and faulty life and from a resolute mind ready to redeem this life. In short, only the committed person is qualified to pray and to meet God. Prayer is always the harbinger of moral reformation.[3]

This is the reason why prayer *per se* does not occupy as prominent a place in the Halakhic community as it does in other faith communities, and why prayer is not the great religious activity claiming, if not exclusiveness, at least centrality. Prayer must always be related to a prayerful life which is consecrated to the realization of the divine imperative, and as such it is not a separate entity, but the sublime prologue to Halakhic action.

IF THE PROPHECY and prayer colloquy is based upon friendship and solidarity nurtured by the "we" consciousness at the experiential as well as the normative level, as a consciousness of both mutual concern and sympathy and of common commitment and determination to bring the divine imperative to full realization, the reverse is also true—that *homo absconditus* cannot reveal himself to his fellow man without joining him in covenantal prayer and moral action. In the natural community which knows no prayer, majestic Adam can offer only his accomplishments, not himself. There is certainly even within the framework of the natural community, as the existentialists are wont to say, a dialogue between the "I" and the "thou." However, this dialogue may only gratify the necessity for communication which urges Adam the first to relate himself to others, since communication for him means information about the surface activity of practical man. Such a dialogue certainly cannot quench the burning thirst for communication in depth of Adam the second, who always will remain a *homo absconditus* if the majestic *logoi* of Adam the first should serve as the only medium of expression. What really can this dialogue reveal of the numinous in-depth personality? Nothing! Yes, words are spoken, but these words reflect not the unique and intimate, but the universal and public in man. As *homo absconditus*, Adam the second is not capable of telling his personal experiential story in majestic formal terms. His emotional life is inseparable from his unique *modus existentiae* and therefore, if communicated to the "thou" only as a piece of surface information, unintelligible. This story belongs exclusively to Adam the second, it is his and only his, and it would make no sense if disclosed to others. Can a sick person afflicted with a fatal disease tell the "thou," who happens to be a very dear and close friend, the tale of a horror-stricken mind confronted with the dreadful prospect of death? Can a parent explain to a rebellious child, who rejects everything the parent stands for, his deep-seated love for him? Distress and bliss, joys and frustrations are incommunicable within the framework of the natural dialogue consisting of common words. By the time *homo absconditus* manages to deliver the message, the personal and intimate content of the latter is already recast in the lingual matrix, which standardizes the unique and universalizes the individual.

If God had not joined the community of Adam and Eve, they would have never been able and would have never cared to make the paradoxical leap over the gap, indeed abyss, separating two individuals whose personal experiential messages are written in a private code undecipherable by anyone else. Without the covenantal experience of the prophetic or prayerful colloquy, Adam *absconditus* would have persisted in his he-role and Eve *abscondita* in her she-role, unknown to and distant from each other. Only when God emerged from the transcendent darkness of He-anonymity into the illumined spaces of community knowability and charged man with an ethical and moral mission, did Adam *absconditus* and Eve *abscondita*, while revealing themselves to God in prayer and in unqualified commitment, also reveal themselves to each other in sympathy and love on the one hand and in common action on the other. Thus, the final objective of the human quest for redemption was attained; the individual felt relieved from loneliness and isolation. The community of the committed became, *ipso facto*, a community of friends—not of neighbors or acquaintances. Friendship—not as a social surface-relation but as an existential in-depth-relation between two individuals—is realizable only within the framework of the covenantal community, where in-depth personalities relate themselves to each other ontologically and total commitment to God and fellow man is the order of the day. In the majestic community, in which surface personalities meet and commitment never exceeds the bounds of the utilitarian, we may find collegiality, neighborliness, civility, or courtesy— but not friendship, which is the exclusive experience awarded by God to covenantal man, who is thus redeemed from his agonizing solitude.

LET US GO FURTHER. The existential insecurity of Adam the second stems, to a great extent, also from his tragic role as a temporal being. He simply cannot pinpoint his position within the rushing stream of time. He knows of an endless past which rolled on without him. He is aware also of an endless future which will rush on with no less force long after he will cease to exist. The link between the "before" in which he was not involved and the "after" from which he will be excluded is the present moment, which vanishes before it is experienced. In fact, the whole accidental character of his being is tied up with this frightening time-consciousness. He began to exist at a certain point—the significance of which he cannot grasp— and his existence will end at another equally arbitrary point. Adam the second experiences the transience and evanescence of a "now" existence which is not warranted either by the "before" or the "after."

Majestic man is not confronted with this time dilemma. The time with which he works and which he knows is quantified, spatialized, and measured, belonging to a cosmic coordinate system. Past and future are not two experiential realities. They just represent two horizontal directions. "Before" and "after" are understandable only within the framework of the causal sequence of events.* Majestic man lives in micro-units of clock time, moving with ease from "now" to "now," completely unaware of a "before" or an "after." Only Adam the second, to whom time is an all-enveloping personal experience, has to cope with the tragic and paradoxical implied in it.

In the covenantal community man of faith finds deliverance from his isolation in the "now," for the latter contains both the "before" and the "after." Every covenantal time experience is both retrospective, reconstructing and reliving the bygone, as well as prospective, anticipating the "about to be."

---

*It is quite characteristic that Aristotle, the man of science, derived time from motion, while Plotinus, the philosopher-mystic— even though, as a pagan, unaware of the idea of the covenant— reversed the order. Of course, for Aristotle, even though he knows of three kinds of motion, the highest is related mainly to morphological change, the transition from possibility to actuality.

In retrospect, covenantal man re-experiences the rendezvous with God in which the covenant, as a promise, hope, and vision, originated. In prospect, he beholds the full eschatological realization of this covenant, its promise, hope, and vision. Let us not forget that the covenantal community includes the "He" who addresses Himself to man not only from the "now" dimension but also from the supposedly already vanished past, from the ashes of a dead "before" facticity as well as from the as yet unborn future, for all boundaries establishing "before," "now," and "after" disappear when God the Eternal speaks. Within the covenantal community not only contemporary individuals but generations are engaged in a colloquy, and each single experience of time is three-dimensional, manifesting itself in memory, actuality, and anticipatory tension. This experiential triad, translated into moral categories, results in an awesome awareness of responsibility to a great past which handed down the divine imperative to the present generation in trust and confidence and to a mute future expecting this generation to discharge its covenantal duty conscientiously and honorably. The best illustration of such a paradoxical time awareness, which involves the individual in the historic performances of the past and makes him also participate in the dramatic action of an unknown future, can be found in the

Judaic *masorah* community. The latter represents not only a formal succession within the framework of calendaric time but the union of the three grammatical tenses in an all-embracing time experience. The *masorah* community cuts across the centuries, indeed millennia, of calendaric time and unites those who already played their part, delivered their message, acquired fame, and withdrew from the covenantal stage quietly and humbly with those who have not yet been given the opportunity to appear on the covenantal stage and who wait for their turn in the anonymity of the "about to be."

Thus, the individual member of the covenantal faith community feels rooted in the past and related to the future. The "before" and the "after" are interwoven in his time experience. He is not a hitchhiker suddenly invited to get into a swiftly traveling vehicle which emerged from nowhere and from which he will be dropped into the abyss of timelessness while the vehicle will rush on into parts unknown, continually taking on new passengers and dropping the old ones. Covenantal man begins to find redemption from insecurity and to feel at home in the continuum of time and responsibility which is experienced by him in its endless totality.* מעולם ועד עולם, from everlasting even to

---

*In reality there are no pure typological structures and hence the

everlasting. He is no longer an evanescent being. He is rooted in everlasting time, in eternity itself. And so covenantal man confronts not only a transient contemporary "thou" but countless "thou" generations which advance toward him from all sides and engage him in the great colloquy in which God Himself participates with love and joy.

This act of revelation does not avail itself of universal speech, objective logical symbols, or metaphors. The message communicated from Adam to Eve certainly consists of words. However, words do not always have to be identified with sound.* It is rather a soundless revelation accomplished in

---

covenantal and majestic communities overlap. Therefore, it is not surprising that we come across the three-dimensional time experience, which we have presented as typically covenantal, in the majestic community as well. The historical community rests, in fact, upon this peculiar time experience. What is historical belonging if not the acceptance of the past as a reality to which one is indebted and the anticipation of a future to which one is responsible? Historical action is never confined to the "now." It crosses the frontiers of perceptible time and relates itself to a unitary experience of time embracing the "before" and the "after." If the stream of time be broken down into micro-units, there would be no place for history. Living in history means experiencing the total drama of history stretching across calendaric time. This peculiarity of the historical experience was known to E. Burke and E. Renan. However, this time awareness was borrowed by majestic history from covenantal history.

* אמר in Hebrew means both to say and to think.

---

muteness and in the stillness of the covenantal community when God responds to the prayerful outcry of lonely man and agrees to meet him as brother and friend, while man, in turn, assumes the great burden which is the price he pays for his encounter with God.

1. The popular Biblical term *tefillah* (prayer) and the esoteric Halakhic term *avodah shebelev* (service of the heart) refer to an inner activity, to a state of mind. *Kavvanah* (intention), related to prayer, is, unlike the *kavvanah* concerning other *mitzvah* (good-deed) performances, not an extraneous addendum but the very core of prayer. The whole Halakhic controversy about *kavvanah* vis-à-vis other *mitzvot* has no relevance to prayer. There is not a single opinion that the latter can be divorced from *kavvanah*. Moreover, the substance of the *kavvanah* as far as prayer is concerned differs fundamentally from that which some require during the performance of other *mitzvot*. While the former denotes a state of mind, an all-embracing awareness of standing before the Almighty, the latter manifests itself only in the normative intention on the part of the *mitzvah*-doer to act in accordance with the will of God. *Kavvanah* in both cases, of course, expresses direction or aiming. However, in prayer one must direct his whole self toward God whereas in the case of other *mitzvot* the directing is confined to a single act. Vide *Berakhot* 28b, 30a-b, 32b, 33a; *Sanhedrin* 22a; Maimonides, *Hilkhot Tefillah*, IV, 16; V, 4. The fact that *kavvanah* is indispensable only for the first benediction of the Silent Prayer does not contradict our premise. The Halakhah simply took into consideration human weakness and inability to immerse in the covenantal awareness for a long time and, in sympathy with the worshiper who is incapable of sustaining a continuous contemplative mood, related the initial *kavvanah* to the entire *Tefillah*. Vide *Berakhot* 34b and *Chidushe R. Hayyim Halevi*, *Tefillah*, IV, 1.

2. The Halakhic requirements of סמיכת גאולה לתפלה, that the recitation of *Shema* with its benedictions be joined to the recital of *Tefillah*, the "Eighteen Benedictions," is indicative of this idea. One has no right to appear before the Almighty without accepting previously all the covenantal commitments implied in the three sections of *Shema*. Vide *Berakhot* 9b and 29b. Both explanations in Rashi, *Berakhot* 4b, actually express the same idea. Vide *Berakhot* 14b and 15a, where it is stated that the reading of *Shema* and the prayers is an integrated act of accepting the Kingdom of Heaven in the most complete manner. It should nevertheless be pointed out that the awareness required by the Halakhah during the recital of the first verse of *Shema* and that which accompanies the act of praying (the recital of the first benediction) are related to two different ideas. During the recital of *Shema* man ideally feels totally committed to God and his awareness is related to a normative end, assigning to man ontological legitimacy and worth as an ethical being whom God charged with a great mission and who is conscious of his freedom either to succeed or to fail in that mission. On the other hand, the awareness which comes with prayer is rooted in man's experiencing his "creatureliness" (to use a term coined by Rudolf Otto) and the absurdity embedded in his own existence. In contrast to the *Shema* awareness, the *Tefillah* awareness negates the legitimacy and worth of human existence. Man, as a slave of God, is completely dependent upon Him. Man enjoys no freedom. "Behold, as the eyes of servants unto the hand of their master, as the eyes of a maiden unto the hand of her mistress, so our eyes look unto the Lord our God until He be gracious unto us."

When the Talmud (*Berakhot* 14b and 15a) speaks of קבלת מלכות שמים שלמה, the unitary acceptance of the Kingdom of God, it refers to the two awarenesses which, notwithstanding their antithetic character, merge into one comprehensive awareness of man who is at the same time the free messenger of God and His captive as well.

However, whether the awareness of prayer *per se* is, from a Halakhic viewpoint, to be construed as קבלת מלכות שמים, as an act of acceptance of the Kingdom of Heaven, is discussed in another passage; see *Berakhot* 21a and Rashi there.

3. The interrelatedness of prayer, moral life, and repentance was emphasized already in Solomon's prayer, I Kings 8:34–51; II Chronicles 7:36–40. See also *Exodus Rabbah*, XXII:3: "Just as they purified their hearts and uttered Song . . . so must a man purify his heart and then pray. . . . This is what Job said: 'Although there is no violence in my hands and my prayer is pure' (15:7). Rabbi Joshua the priest the son of R. Nechemiah said: 'Is there, then, an impure prayer? No; but he who prays unto God with hands soiled from violence is not answered. . . .' Rabbi Chama b. Chanina said 'whence do we know that the prayer of one who has committed violence is impure? Because it says, "And when you spread forth your hands . . . I will not hear because your hands are full of blood." Whence do we know that the prayer of him who removes himself from violence is pure? Because it says . . .' "; Saadya, *Emunot Ve-Deot*, V:6. Also Maimonides, discussing the precept of prayer during times of crisis, says in unequivocal terms that prayer is only the medium through which man may normally rehabilitate himself, although with regard to daily prayer he omitted mention of this relationship. Vide *Ta'anit* I, 1–3; *Tefillah*, IV. It is worthy of note that there is a double discrepancy between the Talmud (*Berakhot* 32b) and the above-quoted Midrash. The Talmud confined the verse of Isaiah 1:15 to the sin of murder which disqualifies the priest from imparting the priestly blessing. The Midrash extended it to all kinds of violence (embezzlement or other corrupt practices) and barred not only priests from blessing the community but all people from prayer.

In my opinion, the discrepancy is only a single one, pertaining to the meaning of the phrase "your hands are full of blood," whether it be limited to murder or extended to all acts of dishonesty and corruption. However, there is no contradiction between the two interpretations as far as extending the applicability of the verse to *Tefillah*; nor could there be, since, in the latter part of the verse, Isaiah himself explicitly mentions *Tefillah*—

"Yea, when ye make prayers, I will not hear." However, the Talmud and the Midrash treated the verse of Isaiah at two different levels. While the Talmud speaks in formal Halakhic categories, the Midrash places it in a metaphysico-moral perspective. The Talmud treats the problem of disqualification; whoever committed murder forfeits the priestly prerogative and right to bless the people. In Halakhic terms, I would say that murder results in a פסול גברא, in the emergence of a personal inadequacy. Indeed, in Maimonides' view, it is not the moral culpability for the sin of murder but the bare fact of being the agent and instrument of murder which causes this disqualification. Hence, the disqualification persists even after the murderer has repented; vide *Tefillah*, XV, 3, and Tosafot, *Menachot* 109a. Such a disqualification is inapplicable to prayer. The privilege and right of prayer cannot be denied to anyone, not even to the most wicked. The Psalmist already stated that everyone is admitted to the realm of prayer: שומע תפלה עדיך כל בשר יבאו "O Thou who hearkenest to prayer; unto Thee doth all flesh come." (Even drunkenness does not disqualify the person, but nullifies the act of prayer because of the lack of *kavvanah*; see Maimonides, *Tefillah* 4, 17.) In fact, the Midrash never stated that a sinner has been stripped of the privilege of prayer. It only emphasized that prayer requires a clean heart and that the prayer of a sinful person is imperfect. The Midrash employs the terms תפלתו זכה and תפלתו עכורה, which denote pure and impure prayer. Maimonides quoted the Midrash not in the section on *Tefillah*, which deals with the Halakhic requirements of prayer, but in that of *Teshuvah*, which deals with the metaphysical as well as the Halakhic aspects of repentance, where he says distinctly that the immoral person's prayer is not fully acceptable to God— צועק ואינו נענה שנאמר גם כי תרבו תפלה אינני שומע "He petitions and is not answered, as it is written, 'Yea, even ye make many prayers I will not hear.' " As a matter of fact, Maimonides extended the requirement for moral excellence to all *mitzvah* performances— עושה מצוות ומורפין אותן בפניו "He performs *mitzvot* and they are thrown back in his face." It is of course self-evident that the imperfection inherent in the deed does not completely nullify the objective worth

77

of the deed. Maimonides' statement at the end of *Tefillah* "that you do not prevent the wicked person from doing a good deed" is not only Halakhically but also psychologically relevant. We let the sinful priest, as long as he has not committed murder or apostasy, impart his blessings to the congregation. Likewise, we encourage the sinner to pray even though he is not ready yet for repentance and moral regeneration, because any *mitzvah* performance, be it prayer, be it another moral act, has a cleansing effect upon the doer and may influence his life and bring about a complete change in his personality. Vide also, Introduction to *Beth Halevi* on Genesis and Exodus.

In Saadya's enumeration of the reasons which prevent prayer from being accepted we find a mixture of Halakhic and metaphysical considerations. The first reason for the rejection of prayer is of a purely metaphysical nature: one's prayer is not answered if it is offered "after the decree was issued against" the person. As an illustration, Saadya introduces the case of Moses beseeching the Lord to allow him to cross the Jordan and not being answered. On the other hand, the second reason—the lack of sincere intention—is Halakhic. It is, therefore, hard to determine whether the five reasons which are related to moral impurity are classified as Halakhic or metaphysical deterrents to prayer.

# VIII

HAVING ARRIVED at this point, we begin to see the lines of the destiny of the man of faith converge. The man of faith, as we explained previously, is lonely because of his being himself exclusively and not having a comrade, a "duplicate I." The man of faith, we further brought out, finds redemption in the covenantal faith community by dovetailing his accidental existence with the necessary infinite existence of the Great True Real Self. There, we pointed out, *homo absconditus* turns into *homo revelatus* vis-à-vis God and man as well.

However, the element of the tragic is not fully eliminated from the destiny of the man of faith even after joining the covenantal community. We said at the very beginning of this essay that the loneliness of the man of faith is an integral part of his destiny from which he can never be completely liberated. The dialectical awareness, the steady oscillating between the majestic natural community and the covenantal faith community renders the act of complete redemption unrealizable. The man of faith, in his continuous movement between the pole of natural majesty and that of covenantal humility, is prevented from totally immersing in the immediate covenantal awareness of the redeeming presence, knowability, and involvement of God in the community of man. From time to time the man of faith is thrown into the majestic community where the colloquy as well as the covenantal consciousness are swept away. He suddenly finds himself revolving around the cosmic center, now and then catching a glimpse of the Creator who hides behind the boundless drama of creation. To be sure, this alternation of cosmic and covenantal involvement is not one of "light and shade," enhanced activity and fatigue, as the mystics are accustomed to call their alternating experiences, but represents two kinds of creative and spontaneous activity, both willed and sanctioned by God.*

*Man's dialectical seesawing between the cosmic and the covenantal experience of God is reflected in the benediction formula in which we address God in both the second and third person. See Nachmanides, Exodus 15:26, and R. Shlomo b. Aderet, *Responsa*, V, 52. To be sure, the mingling of grammatical persons is quite normal in Hebrew syntax. In this case, however, our medieval scholars attributed particular philosophical significance to the change.

Let us not forget that the majestic community is willed by God as much as the covenantal faith community. He wants man to engage in the pursuit of majesty-dignity as well as redemptiveness. He summoned man to retreat from peripheral, hard-won positions of vantage and power to the center of the faith experience. He also commanded man to advance from the covenantal center to the cosmic periphery and recapture the positions he gave up a while ago. He authorized man to quest for "sovereignty"; He also told man to surrender and be totally committed. He enabled man to interpret the world in functional, empirical "how" categories to explain, for instance, the sequence of phenomena in terms of transeunt, mechanical causality and a quantified-spatialized, basically (if not for the law of entropy) reversible time, suitable to the human majestic role. Simultaneously, He also requires of man to forget his functional and bold approach, to stand in humility and dread before the *mysterium magnum* surrounding him, to interpret the world in categories of purposive activity instead of those of mechanical facticity, and to substitute time, wedded to eternity, stretching from *archē* to *eschatos*, for uniform, measured clock-time.

On the one hand, the Bible commands man, "And thou shalt love the Lord thy God with all thy heart and with all thy soul and with all thy

might," a performance of which only covenantal
man is capable since he alone possesses the talent
for complete concentration upon and immersion in
the focus without being distracted by peripheral
interests, anxieties, and problems. On the other
hand, the same Bible which just enjoined man to
withdraw from the periphery to the center commands him to return to the majestic community
which, preoccupied with peripheral interests, anxieties, and problems, builds, plants, harvests, reg-
ulates rivers, heals the sick, participates in state
affairs, is imaginative in dreaming, bold in plan-
ning, daring in undertaking and is out to "conquer"
the world. With what simplicity, not paying the
least attention to the staggering dialectic implied in
such an approach, the Bible speaks of an existence
this-worldly centered—"When thou buildest a new
home; when thou cuttest down thine harvest; when
thou comest into thy neighbor's vineyard"—yet
theo-oriented and unqualifiedly committed to an
eternal purpose! If one would inquire of me about
the teleology of the Halakhah, I would tell him
that it manifests itself exactly in the paradoxical
yet magnificent dialectic which underlies the Halakhic gesture. When man gives himself to the
covenantal community the Halakhah reminds him
that he is also wanted and needed in another
community, the cosmic-majestic, and when it

comes across man while he is involved in the creative enterprise of the majestic community, it does not let him forget that he is a covenantal being who will never find self-fulfillment outside of the covenant and that God awaits his return to the covenantal community.* I would also add, in reply to such a question, that many a time I have the distinct impression that the Halakhah considered the steady oscillating of the man of faith between majesty and covenant not as a dialectical but rather as a complementary movement. The majestic gesture of the man of faith, I am inclined to think, is looked upon by the Halakhah not as contradictory to the covenantal encounter but rather as the reflex action which is caused by this encounter when man feels the gentle touch of God's hand upon his shoulder and the covenantal invitation to join God is extended to him. I am prompted to draw this

---

*Not only Halakhic teleology but also positive Halakhic thinking is dialectical. The latter follows the rules of an N-valued logic rather than those of a two-valued logic. Positive Halakhah has never honored the sacrosanct classical principle of the excluded middle or that of contradiction. Quite often it has predicated of $x$ that it is neither $a$ nor $b$ or that it is both $a$ and $b$ at the same time.

It is worth mentioning that it took scientific thinking a very long time to make the discovery that the complex cosmic occurrence does not lend itself to a two-valued logical interpretation. [The role of multivalued logic in Halakhah is discussed by Rabbi Soloveitchik in *The Halakhic Mind* (New York: Free Press, 1986).]

---

remarkable inference from the fact that the Halakhah has a monistic approach to reality and has unreservedly rejected any kind of dualism. The Halakhah believes that there is only one world— not divisible into secular and hallowed sectors— which can either plunge into ugliness and hatefulness, or be roused to meaningful, redeeming activity, gathering up all latent powers into a state of holiness. Accordingly, the task of covenantal man is to be engaged not in dialectical surging forward and retreating, but in uniting the two communities into one community where man is both the creative, free agent, and the obedient servant of God. Notwithstanding the huge disparity between these two communities, which expresses itself in the typological oppositions and conflicts described previously, the Halakhah sees in the ethico-moral norm a uniting force. The norm which originates in the covenantal community addresses itself almost exclusively to the majestic community where its realization takes place. To use a metaphor, I would say that the norm in the opinion of the Halakhah is the tentacle by which the covenant, like the ivy, attaches itself to and spreads over the world of majesty.[1]

THE BIBLICAL DIALECTIC stems from the fact that Adam the first, majestic man of dominion and success, and Adam the second, the lonely man of faith, obedience, and defeat, are not two different people locked in an external confrontation as an "I" opposite a "thou," but one person who is involved in self-confrontation. "I," Adam the first, confront the "I," Adam the second. In every one of us abide two *personae*—the creative, majestic Adam the first, and the submissive, humble Adam the second. As we portrayed them typologically, their views are not commensurate; their methods are different, their modes of thinking, distinct, the categories in which they interpret themselves and their environment, incongruous. Yet, no matter how far-reaching the cleavage, each of us must willy-nilly identify himself with the whole of an all-inclusive human personality, charged with responsibility as both a majestic and a covenantal being. God created two Adams and sanctioned both. Rejection of either aspect of humanity would be tantamount to an act of disapproval of the divine scheme of creation which was approved by God as being very good. As a matter of fact, men of faith have accepted Adam the first a long time ago. Notwithstanding the fact that Adam the second is the bearer of a unique commitment, he remains also a man of majesty who is inspired by the joyous spirit of creativity and constructive adventure.*

*I hardly believe that any responsible man of faith, who is verily

SINCE THE DIALECTICAL ROLE has been assigned to man by God, it is God who wants the man of faith to oscillate between the faith community and the community of majesty, between being confronted by God in the cosmos and the intimate, immediate apprehension of God through the covenant, and who therefore willed that complete human redemption be unattainable.

Had God placed Adam in the majestic community only, then Adam would, as it was stated before, never be aware of existential loneliness. The sole problem would then be that of aloneness—one that majestic Adam could resolve. Had God, vice versa, thrust Adam into the covenantal community exclusively, then he would be beset by the passional experience of existential loneliness and also provided with the means of finding redemption from this experience through his covenantal relation to God and to his fellow man. However, God, in His inscrutable wisdom, has decreed differ-

interested in the destiny of his community and wants to see it thriving and vibrant, would recommend now the philosophy of *contemptus saeculi*. I believe that even within the classical medieval tradition the monastic-ascetic approach was just an undercurrent and that the philosophers and moralists moving with the mainstream of religious thought preached the doctrine of human optimism and activism.

ently. Man discovers his loneliness in the covenantal community, and before he is given a chance
to climb up to the high level of a complete covenantal, revealed existence, dedicated in faith to
God and in sympathy to man, man of faith is
pushed into a new community where he is told to
lead an expanded surface existence rather than a
covenantal, concentrated in-depth existence. Because of this onward movement from center to
center, man does not feel at home in any community. He is commanded to move on before he
manages to strike roots in either of these communities and so the ontological loneliness of man of
faith persists. Verily, "A straying Aramean was my
father."*

*Jewish eschatology beholds the great vision of a united majestic-
covenantal community in which all oppositions will be reconciled
and absolute harmony will prevail. When Zechariah proclaimed
"the Lord shall be King over all the earth; on that day the Lord shall
be one and His name one," he referred not to the unity of God,
which is absolute and perfect even now, but to the future unity of
creation, which is currently torn asunder by inner contradictions.
On that distant day the dialectical process will come to a close and
man of faith as well as majestic man will achieve full redemption in
a united world.

1. *Vide Berakhot* 35b; *Shabbat* 33b. Maimonides distinguishes between two kinds of dialectic: (1) the constant oscillating between the
majestic and the covenantal community; (2) the simultaneous involvement in both communities, which is the highest form of

dialectical existence and which, according to Maimonides, only Moses and the Patriarchs achieved. See *Yesode ha-Torah* VII, 6: "Hence it may be inferred that all prophets when the prophetic power left them returned to their tents, that they attended to the satisfaction of their physical needs. Moses, our teacher, never went back to his former tent. He, accordingly, permanently separated himself from his wife, and abstained from similar gratifications. His mind was closely attached to the Rock of the Universe. . . ." This, however, is not to be interpreted as if Moses had abandoned the majestic community. After all, Moses dedicated his life to the fashioning of a majestic-covenantal community bent on conquest and political-economic normalcy on the one hand, and the realization of the covenantal *kerygma* on the other.

Maimonides is more explicit in the *Moreh*, III, 51 where he portrays the routine of the Patriarchs who, like Moses, achieved the highest form of dialectical existence and resided in both communities concurrently. "The Patriarchs likewise attained this degree of perfection. . . . When we therefore find them also engaged in ruling others, in increasing their property and endeavoring to obtain possession of wealth and honor, we see in this fact a proof that when they were occupied in these things their bodily limbs were at work while their heart and mind never moved away from the name of God. . . ." In other words, the Patriarchs were builders of society, sociable and gregarious. They made friends with whom they participated in the majestic endeavor. However, axiologically, they valued only one involvement: their covenantal friendship with God. The perfect dialectic expresses itself in a plurality of creative gestures and, at the same time, in axiological monoideism.

The concluding paragraphs of *Hilkhot Shemitah Ve-Yovel* should be interpreted in a similar vein. Cf. *Nefesh ha-Chayyim*, II, 11.

The unqualified acceptance of the world of majesty by the Halakhah expresses itself in its natural and inevitable involvement in every sector of human majestic endeavor. There is not a single theoretical or technological discovery, from new psychological insights into the human personality to man's attempts to reach out among the planets, with which the Halakhah is not concerned. New Halakhic problems arise with every new scientific discovery. As a matter of fact, at present, in order to render precise Halakhic decisions in many fields of human endeavor, one must possess, besides excellent Halakhic training, a good working knowledge in those secular fields in which the problem occurs.

This acceptance, easily proven in regard to the total majestic gesture, is most pronounced in the Halakhah's relationship to scientific medicine and the art of healing. The latter has always been considered by the Halakhah as a great and noble occupation. Unlike other faith communities, the Halakhic community has never been troubled by the problem of human interference, on the part of the physician and patient, with God's will. On the contrary, argues the Halakhah, God wants man to fight evil bravely and to mobilize all his intellectual and technological ingenuity in order to defeat it. The conquest of disease is the sacred duty of the man of majesty, and he must not shirk it. From the Biblical phrase "Only he shall pay for the loss of his time and shall cause him to be thoroughly healed" (Exodus 21:18), through the Talmudic period in which scientific medicine was considered authoritative in situations in which the saving of a human life, פיקוח נפש, requires the suspension of the religious law, to the Judeo-Spanish tradition of combining Halakhic scholarship with medical skill, the Halakhah remained steadfast in its loyalty to scientific medicine. It has never ceased to emphasize the duty of the sick person to consult a competent physician. The statement quoted in both the *Tur* and Karo's *Shulchan Aruch*, ואם מונע עצמו הרי זה שופך דמים, "And if he refrains [from consulting a physician], it is as if he shed his own blood," which can be traced indirectly to a Talmudic passage, is a cornerstone of Halakhic thinking. Vide *Yoma* 82a, 82b, 83a; *Kiddushin* 82a; Rashi sub טוב; *Bava Kamma* 85a, Tosafot sub שניתנה; *Tur Yoreh Deah* 336; *Bayit-Chadash* sub תניא. See also *Pesachim* 56a, Rashi and Maimonides' Commentary.

Nachmanides' observation in Leviticus 26:11 refers to an ideal state of the covenantal community enjoying unlimited divine grace and has no application, therefore, to the imperfect state of affairs of the ordinary world.

The passage in II Chronicles 16:12: "yet in his disease he sought not to the Lord, but to physicians" referred to priest-doctors who employed pagan rites and magic in order to "heal" the sick.

The doctrine of faith in God's charity, בטחון , is not to be equated with the folly of the mystical doctrine of quietism, which in its extreme form exempts man from his duty of attending to his own needs and lets him wait in "holy" idleness and indifference for God's intervention. This kind of repose is wholly contrary to the repose which the Halakhah recommends: the one which follows human effort and remedial action. Man must first use his own skill and try to help himself as much as possible. Then, and only then, man may find repose and quietude in God and be confident that his effort and action will be crowned with success. The initiative, says the Halakhah, belongs to man; the successful realization, to God.

Certainly, "except the Lord build the house, they labor in vain that build it," but if those who labor stop building, there will be no house. The Lord wants man to undertake the task which He, in His infinite grace, completes.

# IX

WHILE THE ontological loneliness of the man of faith is due to a God-made and willed situation and is, as part of his destiny, a wholesome and integrating experience, the special kind of loneliness of contemporary man of faith referred to at the beginning of this essay is of a social nature due to a manmade historical situation and is, hence, an unwholesome and frustrating experience.

Let me diagnose the situation in a few terse sentences. Contemporary Adam the first, extremely successful in his cosmic-majestic enterprise, refuses to pay earnest heed to the duality in man and tries to deny the undeniable, that another Adam exists beside or, rather, in him. By rejecting Adam the second, contemporary man, *eo ipso*, dismisses the covenantal faith community as something superfluous and obsolete. To clear up any misunderstanding on the part of my audience, I wish to note that I am not concerned in this essay with the vulgar and illiterate atheism professed and propagated in the most ugly fashion by a natural-political community which denies the unique transcendental worth of the human personality. I am referring rather to Western man who is affiliated with organized religion and is a generous supporter of its institutions. He stands today in danger of losing his dialectical awareness and of abandoning completely the metaphysical polarity implanted in man as a member of both the majestic and the covenantal community. Somehow, man of majesty considers the dialectical awareness too great a burden, interfering with his pursuit of happiness and success, and is, therefore, ready to cast it off.

LET US TRY to describe in brief the philosophy by which successful Western man is guided in his appraisal of his transcendental commitment.

I said a while ago that I am speaking of Western man who belongs and extends help to some religious establishment. Nevertheless, no matter how conscientious and devoted a fellow member he is, he belongs not to a covenantal faith community but to a religious community. The two communities are as far apart as the two Adams. While the covenantal faith community is governed, as I emphasized, by a desire for a redeemed existence, the religious community is dedicated to the attainment of dignity and success and is—along with the whole gamut of communities such as the political, the scientific, the artistic—a creation of Adam the first, all conforming to the same sociological structural patterns. The religious community is, therefore, also a work community consisting of two grammatical *personae* not including the Third Person. The prime purpose is the successful furtherance of the interests, not the deepening and enhancing of the commitments, of man who values religion in terms of its usefulness to him and considers the religious act a medium through which he may increase his happiness. This assumption on the part of majestic man about the role of religion is not completely wrong, if only, as I shall explain, he would recognize also the nonpragmatic aspects of religion. Faith is indeed relevant to man not only metaphysically but also practically. It gives his life, even at the secular mundane level, a new existential dimension. Certain aspects of the doctrinal and normative covenantal *kerygma* of faith are of utmost importance to majestic man and are, in a paradoxical way, translatable into the latter's vernacular. It is very certain and self-evident that Adam the first cannot succeed completely in his efforts to attain majesty-dignity without having the man of faith contribute his share. The cultural edifice whose great architect Adam the first is would be built on shifting sands if he sought to conceal from himself and from others the fact that he alone cannot implement the mandate of majesty-dignity entrusted to him by God and that he must petition Adam the second for help. To be sure, man can build spaceships capable of reaching other planets without addressing himself to the mystery of faith and without being awakened to an enhanced, inspired life which reflects the covenantal truth. He certainly can triumph to a limited degree over the elemental forces of nature without crossing the frontiers of here-and-now sense-facticity. The Tower of Babel can be built high and mighty without beholding and acknowledging the great verity that Heaven is yet higher. However, the idea of majesty which Adam the first is striving to realize embraces much more than the mere building of machines, no matter how complex and efficacious. Successful man wants to be a sovereign not only in the physical but also in the spiritual world. He is questing not only for material success, but for ideological and axiological achievements as well. He is concerned with a philosophy of nature and man, of matter and mind, of things and ideas.

Adam the first is not only a creative mind,

incessantly looking and pressing forward, but also a meditating mind, casting a backward glance and appraising his handiwork, thereby imitating his Maker who, at the end of each stage of creation, inspected and appraised it. Adam frequently interrupts his forward march, turns around, views and evaluates his creative accomplishments, making an effort to place them in some philosophical and axiological perspective.

Furthermore, as I commented previously, Adam distinguishes himself not only in the realm of scientific theory but in that of the ethico-moral and aesthetic gestures as well. He legislates norms which he invests with validity and great worth. He fashions beautiful forms and considers the encounter with them ennobling and cleansing, exhilarating and enriching. All this Adam the first seeks, yet he is not always lucky to find it. For the retrospective appraisal and appreciation of the cognitive drama as well as the successful performance at the ethico-moral and aesthetic levels are unattainable as long as man moves continuously within the closed, vicious cycle of the insensate natural occurrence and never reaches for the "beyond." To take an illustration, the parallelism between *cogitatio* and *existentia*, between the pure logical constructs of the mind and the real dynamics of nature, on which modern science rests and which troubles the meditating mind of Adam the first, will remain a mystery as long as he will not admit that these two parallel lines of thought and facticity converge in infinity within the True, Real Self. In like manner, the worth and validity of the ethical norm, if it is born of the finite creative-social gesture of Adam the first, cannot be upheld. Only the sanctioning by a higher moral will is capable of lending to the norm fixity, permanence, and worth. Likewise, majestic man is quite often in need of the redemptive and therapeutic powers inherent in the act of believing which, in times of crisis, may give aid and comfort to the distressed mind. In similar fashion, the aesthetic experience to which contemporary man abandons himself with almost mystical ecstasy remains incomplete as long as beauty does not rise to sublimity and remains unredeemed. However, redemption is a covenantal category and the sublime is inseparable from the exalted. And how can majestic man be confronted with redeemed beauty in which the exalted is reflected if he is enclosed in a dreary mechanical world from which he has neither strength nor courage to free himself? In short, the message of faith, if translated into cultural categories, fits into the axiological and philosophical frame of reference of the creative cultural consciousness and is pertinent even to secular man.

For good reason did the thinkers throughout the centuries speak of philosophical religion which emanates from the deep recesses of the human personality. They knew very well that the human, creative, cultural gesture is incomplete if it does not relate itself to a higher *modus existentiae*. No wonder that the Kantian and neo-Kantian philosophies, scientific and empirical as they are, let the creative cultural consciousness pick out from the flow of transient impressions, abstract constructs, and ideas those bits that point toward the infinite and eternal. From these elements they tried to construct a pure, rational religious awareness in order to endow the whole creative gesture with intrinsic worth and with ultimate and unconditioned validity.* Since majestic man is in need of a transcendental experience in order to strengthen his cultural edifice, it is the duty of the man of

*According to Kant, the need for a rational metaphysics is constantly reasserted by the pure reason even though the latter cannot gratify this need. However, what the pure reason cannot achieve is accomplished by the practical reason or the moral will which is an integral part of the free, creative cultural consciousness. The three postulates of the moral will—freedom, God, and immortality—have very little in common with the covenantal doctrine pertaining to these postulates. They are pure, rational ideas which make the ethical performance meaningful. In other words, the need for religion is part of the all-inclusive human need for cultural self-expression.

faith to provide him with some component parts of this experience. God would not have implanted the necessity in majestic man for such spiritual perceptions and ideas if He had not at the same time endowed the man of faith with the skill of converting some of his apocalyptic experiences—which are meta-logical and nonhedonic—into a system of values and verities comprehensible to majestic man, the experimenter, aesthete, and, above all, the creative mind.

AT THIS POINT, however, the crisis in the relations between man of faith and majestic man begins to develop. If the job of translating faith mysteries into cultural aspects could be fully accomplished, then contemporary man of faith could free himself, if not from the ontological awareness which is perennial, then, at least, from the peculiar feeling of psychological loneliness and anguish which is due to his historical confrontation with the man of culture. The man of faith would, if this illusion came true, be at peace with the man of culture so that the latter would fully understand the significance of human dialectics, and a perfect harmonious relationship would prevail between both Adams.*

*The idea that certain aspects of faith are translatable into

However, this harmony can never be attained since the man of faith is not the compromising type and his covenantal commitment eludes cognitive analysis by the *logos* and hence does not lend itself completely to the act of cultural translation. There are simply no cognitive categories in which the total commitment of the man of faith could be spelled out. This commitment is rooted not in one dimension, such as the rational one, but in the whole personality of the man of faith. The whole of the human being, the rational as well as the non-rational aspects, is committed to God. Hence, the magnitude of the commitment is beyond the comprehension of the *logos* and the *ethos*. The act of faith is aboriginal, exploding with elemental force as an all-consuming and all-pervading eudaemonic-passional experience in which our most secret urges, aspirations, fears, and passions, at times even unsuspected by us, manifest themselves. The commitment of the man of faith is thrown into the mold of the in-depth personality and immediately accepted before the mind is given a chance to investigate the reasonableness of this unqualified

pragmatic terms is not new. The Bible has already pointed out that the observance of the Divine Law and obedience to God lead man to worldly happiness, to a respectable, pleasant, and meaningful life. Religious pragmatism has a place within the perspective of the man of faith.

commitment. The intellect does not chart the course of the man of faith; its role is an *a posteriori* one. It attempts, *ex post facto*, to retrace the footsteps of the man of faith, and even in this modest attempt the intellect is not completely successful. Of course, as long as the path of the man of faith cuts across the territory of the reasonable, the intellect may follow him and identify his footsteps. The very instant, however, the man of faith transcends the frontiers of the reasonable and enters into the realm of the unreasonable, the intellect is left behind and must terminate its search for understanding. The man of faith animated by his great experience is able to reach the point at which not only his logic of the mind but even his logic of the heart and of the will, everything—even his own "I" awareness—has to give in to an "absurd" commitment. The man of faith is "insanely" committed to and "madly" in love with God.[1]

"Stay ye me with dainties, refresh me with apples, for I am lovesick."*

---

*Vide* Maimonides, *Hilkhot Teshuvah*, X, 3. "What is the love of God that is befitting? It is to love the Eternal with a great and exceeding love, so strong that one's soul shall be knit up with the love of God, and one should be continually enraptured by it, like a lovesick individual whose mind is at no time free from its passion. . . ."

THE UNTRANSLATABILITY of the complete faith experience is due not to the weakness, but to the greatness of the latter.

If an all-embracing translation of the great mystery of revelation and its *kerygma* were possible, then the uniqueness of the faith experience and its commitments would be lost. Only peripheral elements of the act of faith can be projected on a cognitive, pragmatic background. Prayer, for instance, might appeal to majestic man as the most uplifting, integrating, and purifying act, arousing the finest and noblest emotions, yet these characteristics, however essential to Adam the first, are of marginal interest to Adam the second, who experiences prayer as the awesome confrontation of God and man, as the great paradox of man conversing with God as an equal fellow member of the covenantal society, and at the same time being aware that he fully belongs to God and that God demands complete surrender and self-sacrifice.

There is, of course, an amazing parallelism between the cultural experience and the apocalyptic one. Yet, I repeat, no matter how impressive the similarities are, the act of faith is unique and cannot be fully translated into cultural categories.

In a word, the message of translated religion is not the only one which the man of faith must address to majestic man of culture. Besides this message, man of faith must bring to the attention of man of culture the *kerygma* of original faith in all its singularity and pristine purity, in spite of the incompatibility of this message with the fundamental credo of a utilitarian society. How staggering this incompatibility is! This unique message speaks of defeat instead of success, of accepting a higher will instead of commanding, of giving instead of conquering, of retreating instead of advancing, of acting "irrationally" instead of being always reasonable. Here the tragic event occurs. Contemporary majestic man rejects his dialectical assignment and, with it, the man of faith.

The situation has deteriorated considerably in this century, which has witnessed the greatest triumphs of majestic man in his drive for conquest. Majestic Adam has developed a demonic quality: laying claim to unlimited power—alas, to infinity itself. His pride is almost boundless, his imagination arrogant, and he aspires to complete and absolute control of everything. Indeed, like the men of old, he is engaged in constructing a tower whose apex should pierce Heaven. He is intoxicated with his own adventures and victories and is bidding for unrestricted dominion. In order to avoid misinterpretation, let me say that I am not referring here to man's daring experiments in space. From a religious point of view, as I said before, they are quite legitimate and in compliance with the divine testament given to Adam the first that he should rule nature. When I say that modern man is projecting a demonic image, I am thinking of man's attempt to dominate himself, or, to be more precise, of Adam the first's desire to identify himself with the total human personality, declaring his creative talents as ultimate, ignoring completely Adam the second and his preoccupation with the unique and strange transcendental experience which resists subservience to the cultural interests of majestic man. Notwithstanding the fact that Western man is in a nostalgic mood, he is determined not to accept the dialectical burden of humanity. He certainly feels spiritually uprooted, emotionally disillusioned, and, like the old king of Ecclesiastes, is aware of his own tragedy. Yet this pensive mood does not arouse him to heroic action. He, of course, comes to a place of worship. He attends lectures on religion and appreciates the ceremonial, yet he is searching not for a faith in all its singularity and otherness, but for religious culture. He seeks not the greatness found in sacrificial action but the convenience one discovers in a comfortable, serene state of mind. He is desirous of an aesthetic experience rather than a covenantal one, of a social ethos rather than a divine imperative. In a word, he wants to find in faith that which he cannot find in his laboratory, or in the privacy of his luxurious home. His efforts are noble, yet he is not ready for a genuine faith experience which requires the giving of one's self unreservedly to God, who demands unconditional commitment, sacrificial action, and retreat. Western man diabolically insists on being successful. Alas, he wants to be successful even in his adventure with God. If he gives of himself to God, he expects reciprocity. He also reaches a covenant with God, but this covenant is a mercantile one. In a primitive manner, he wants to trade "favors" and exchange goods. The gesture of faith for him is a give-and-take affair and reflects the philosophy of Job which led to catastrophe—a philosophy which sees faith as a *quid pro quo* arrangement and expects compensation for each sacrifice one offers. Therefore, modern man puts up demands that faith adapt itself to the mood and temper of modern times. He does not discriminate between translated religion formulated in cultural categories—which are certainly fluid since they have been evolved by the human creative consciousness—and the pure faith commitment which is as unchangeable as eternity itself. Certainly, when the man of faith interprets his transcendental awareness in cultural categories, he takes advantage of modern interpretive methods and is selective in picking his categories. The cultural message of faith changes, indeed, constantly, with the flow of time, the shifting of the spiritual climate, the fluctuations of axiological moods, and the rise of social needs. However, the act of faith itself is unchangeable, for it transcends the bounds of time and space. Faith is born of the intrusion of eternity upon temporality. Its essence is characterized by fixity and enduring identity. Faith is experienced not as a product of some emergent evolutionary process, or as something which has been brought into existence by man's creative cultural gesture, but as something which was given to man when the latter was overpowered by God. Its prime goal is redemption from the inadequacies of finitude and, mainly, from the flux of temporality. Unfortunately, modern Adam the first refuses to accept this unique message, which would cause him to become involved in the dialectical movement, and he clings instead zealously to his role as majestic man exclusively, demanding the surrender of faith to his transient interests. In his demonic quest for dominion, he forgets that relativization of faith, doctrine, and norm will inflict untold harm upon him and his majestic interests. He fails to realize that the reality of the power of faith, which may set modern man free from anxiety and neurotic complexes and help him plan the strategy of invincible majestic living, can only be experienced if the faith gesture is left alone, outside of the fleeting stream of socio-cultural metamorphoses and tolerated as something stable and immutable. If the faith gesture should be cut loose from its own absolute moorings and allowed to float upon the mighty waters of historical change, then it will forfeit its redemptive and therapeutic qualities.

It is here that the dialogue between the man of faith and the man of culture comes to an end. Modern Adam the second, as soon as he finishes translating religion into the cultural vernacular and begins to talk the "foreign" language of faith, finds himself lonely, forsaken, misunderstood, at times even ridiculed by Adam the first, by himself. When the hour of estrangement strikes, the ordeal of man of faith begins and he starts his withdrawal from society, from Adam the first—be he an outsider, be he himself. He returns, like Moses of old, to his solitary hiding and to the abode of loneliness. Yes, the loneliness of contemporary man of faith is of a special kind. He experiences not only ontological loneliness but also social isolation, whenever he dares to deliver the genuine faith-*kerygma*. This is both the destiny and the human historical situation of the man who keeps a rendezvous with eternity, and who, in spite of everything, continues tenaciously to bring the message of faith to majestic man.

1. Our description of the "individuality" and autonomy of the faith gesture should not be associated with Tertullian's apothegm *credo quia absurdum est*. Neither should it be equated with Kierkegaard's "leap into the absurd."

Tertullian tried not only to free the act of faith from its subservience to the intellect but actually to posit them as two inexorable foes. Thus, he considered any attempt to translate aspects of faith into cultural-majestic categories as illegitimate and negating the very essence of faith. This kind of antirationalism led to complete rejection of majestic man willed and created by God. Small wonder that Tertullian's contemporary Tatian condemned the majestic gesture as the work of the devil.

Tertullian was wrong also in another respect. The terms "reasonable" and "unreasonable" belong exclusively to the realm of the *logos* and are, therefore, inapplicable to the act of faith. Neither does one believe because it is reasonable to do so, since the reasonable is affirmed on logical grounds and is in no need of being affirmed by an act of faith, nor is it sensible to say that one has faith because the latter contradicts human reason. The faith gesture is not motivated by intellectual insights or convictions.

The term "absurd" in the Kierkegaardian philosophy is both a logical and a psychological category. It refers not only to logically false statements but also to unreasonable psychological motivation. The act of "repetition" precipitated by failure and resignation is absurd and belongs, therefore, to the realm of faith. In a word, for Kierkegaard, faith supersedes the majestic posture of man. The world of faith rises upon the ruins and debris of the world of majesty.

This thesis is unacceptable, as we indicated in the text, to the Halakhah, which insists upon the dialectical movement between these two worlds. They do, indeed, exist concurrently according to the Halakhah. Moreover, Kierkegaard lacked the understanding of the centrality of the act of objectification of the inner movement of faith in a normative and doctrinal postulate system, which forms the very foundation of the Halakhah. The Halakhic world of faith is "terribly" articulate, "unpardonably" dynamic, and "foolishly" consistent, insisting that feeling become thought, and that experience be acted out and transformed into an objective event. Kierkegaard's existentialist world, like Schleiermacher's pietistic world, is a place of silence and passivity, far removed from the complex array of historical events, not hungering for action or movement.

# X

*So he departed thence, and found Elisha, the son of Shafat, who was plowing with twelve yoke of oxen before him and he with the twelfth; and Elijah passed by him and cast his mantle upon him. And he left the oxen and ran after Elijah, and said, "let me I pray thee kiss my father and my mother and then I will follow thee," and he said unto him, "go back again for what have I done to thee." And he returned back from him and took a yoke of oxen and slew them, and boiled their flesh with the instruments of the oxen and gave unto the people and they did eat. Then he arose and went after Elijah and ministered unto him. (I Kings, 19:19–21)*

**E**LISHA WAS a typical representative of the majestic community. He was the son of a prosperous farmer, a man of property, whose interests were centered around this-worldly, material goods such as crops, livestock, and market prices. His objective was economic success, his aspiration—material wealth. The Bible portrays him as efficient, capable, and practical, remindful of a modern business executive. When Elijah met him, we are told, he was supervising the work done by the slaves. He was with the twelfth yoke in order not to lose sight of the slave-laborers. What did this man of majesty have in common with Elijah, the solitary covenantal prophet, the champion of God, the adversary of kings, who walked as a stranger through the bustling cities of Shomron, past royal pomp and grandeur, negating the worth of all goods to which his contemporaries were committed, reproaching the sinners, preaching the law of God and portending His wrath? What bond could exist between a complacent farmer who enjoyed his homestead and the man in the hairy dress who came from nowhere and who finally disappeared under a veil of mystery? Yet unexpectedly, the call came through to this unimaginative, self-centered farmer. Suddenly the mantle of Elijah was cast upon him. While he was engaged in the most ordinary, everyday activity, in tilling the soil, he encountered God and felt the transforming touch of God's hand. The strangest metamorphosis occurred. Within seconds, the old Elisha disappeared and a new Elisha emerged.

Majestic man was replaced by covenantal man. He was initiated into a new spiritual universe in which clumsy social-class distinctions had little meaning, wealth played no role, and a serene, illuminated, universal "we" consciousness supplanted the small, limited, and selfish "I" consciousness. Old concerns changed, past commitments vanished, cherished hopes faded, and a new vision of a redemptive-covenantal reality incommensurate with the old vision of an enjoyable-majestic reality beckoned to him. No more did the "farmer" care for the oxen, the means of making the soil yield its abundance, which were so precious to him a while ago. No more was he concerned with anything which was so dear to him before. He slew the oxen and fed the meat to the slaves who, half-starved, tilled the soil for him and whom he, until that meeting with Elijah, had treated with contempt. Moreover, covenantal man renounced his family relationships. He bade farewell to father and mother and departed from their home for good. Like his master, he became homeless. Like his ancestor Jacob he became a "straying Aramean" who took defeat and humiliation with charity and gratitude. However, Elisha's withdrawal from majesty was not final. He followed the dialectical course of all our prophets. Later, when he achieved the pinnacle of faith and arrived at the outer boundaries of human commit-

ment, he came back to society as a participant in
state affairs, as an adviser of kings and a teacher of
the majestic community. God ordered him to return to the people, to offer them a share in the
covenantal drama and to involve them in the great
and solemn colloquy. He was God's messenger
carrying, like Moses, two tablets of stone contain-
ing the covenantal *kerygma*. Many a time he felt
disenchanted and frustrated because his words
were scornfully rejected. However, Elisha never
despaired or resigned. Despair and resignation
were unknown to the man of the covenant who
found triumph in defeat, hope in failure, and who
could not conceal God's Word that was, to paraphrase Jeremiah, deeply implanted in his bones
and burning in his heart like an all-consuming fire.
Elisha was indeed lonely, but in his loneliness he
met the Lonely One and discovered the singular
covenantal confrontation of solitary man and God
who abides in the recesses of transcendental solitude.

Is modern man of faith entitled to a more privileged position and a less exacting and sacrificial
role?

ABOUT THE AUTHOR

JOSEPH B. SOLOVEITCHIK was born in Russia in 1903 into a family of eminent Eastern European rabbis. Initially trained in the scholarship of the sacred texts of Judaism, he enrolled at twenty-two at the University of Berlin in order to study physics, mathematics, and philosophy. He wrote his dissertation on the philosopher Hermann Cohen. In 1932 he accepted the position of chief rabbi of Boston, where he has made his home since. In 1939 he founded the Maimonides School there. For years he commuted to New York City in order to teach at Yeshiva University, where his lectures gained renown for their probity and breadth. He has been regarded throughout the world as the leading authority on the meaning of the Jewish law and the leading intellectual figure in the effort to build bridges between Orthodox Judaism and the modern world.